WHY WR

Collect
the cor

Pete ⁄ ᴕ ᴄᴋ

P

First published in Great Britain in 2016 by

Policy Press
University of Bristol
1-9 Old Park Hill
Bristol
BS2 8BB
UK
t: +44 (0)117 954 5940
pp-info@bristol.ac.uk
www.policypress.co.uk

North America office:
Policy Press
c/o The University of Chicago Press
1427 East 60th Street
Chicago, IL 60637, USA
t: +1 773 702 7700
f: +1 773 702 9756
sales@press.uchicago.edu
www.press.uchicago.edu

© Policy Press 2016

British Library Cataloguing in Publication Data
A catalogue record for this book is available from the British Library

Library of Congress Cataloging-in-Publication Data
A catalog record for this book has been requested

ISBN 978-1-4473-2834-6 paperback
ISBN 978-1-4473-2836-0 ePub
ISBN 978-1-4473-2837-7 Mobi

Cover design by Hayes Design
Printed and bound in Great Britain by CMP, Poole
Policy Press uses environmentally responsible print partners

For Anna and Chris, and Dan and Tom

Contents

List of boxes and figures

Boxes

Figures

About the author

Pete Alcock is Professor of Social Policy and Administration at the University of Birmingham. Pete has taught and researched social policy for over 30 years, moving to Birmingham in 1998, where he has held a number of posts, including Head of the School of Social Sciences and Director of the ESRC Third Sector Research Centre (TSRC). He is author and editor of a number of leading books on social policy, including *The student's companion to social policy* (5th edn, forthcoming, 2016). His research has covered the fields of poverty and anti-poverty policy, social security, and the role of the UK third sector.

Preface and acknowledgements

I was born in 1951. Wartime rationing was still in force and George VI was still on the throne. More importantly, though, following the end of the Second World War, the UK had just been through the most significant period of social reform in its history, culminating in the creation of the welfare state. Like all of my generation I was among the first to grow up with free healthcare, free state education up to age 18, free places at university (although far fewer places than are available now), expanding public and private housing, reducing inequality and a growing economy. Some might say we were lucky; but it was not luck. It was the result of political commitments to make collective investment in public welfare the centrepiece of social and economic planning, and to secure popular support for this through democratic government. And, of course, to a large extent it was what our parents had fought the war to win, for which we remain forever grateful.

At the beginning of the twenty-first century, the welfare state that I enjoyed faces a series of challenges. These are both internal (it has not always proved easy to deliver on the commitments to provide public welfare for all) and external (economic and political changes have questioned the value of such collective investment). In this book I seek to explore these challenges and to explain the impact they have had on the welfare state. But the book is not just about what has happened to the welfare state; it is about what should happen to it in the future. The value of the investment in collective welfare has not been diminished by the challenges that it has faced, and the values that I have acquired through living under its warm glow have made me ever more aware of its enduring importance. It was the legacy my parents' generation left for me; I believe it is important that my children enjoy a similar legacy. This book is about why that legacy remains so important, and how we might work to provide it. It is dedicated to my children, and all of their generation, in the hope that they too can continue to share in our common good.

I should especially like to thank Sandra Cooke for encouraging me to write this book in the first place and for her perceptive and supportive comments on some of the early drafts. She was a source of inspiration and support throughout. I am grateful for the support provided by Policy Press and the advice from their anonymous reviewers. And I should like to thank the University of Birmingham for providing some study time for me to work on the writing. For the final content, however, I am happy to accept all responsibility.

I would like to thank John Hills and Policy Press for permission to reproduce Figure 2.5 from Hills, J. (2015) *Good times, bad times: The welfare myth of them and us*, Bristol: Policy Press.

1

Introduction

The importance of collective action

This book sets out the case for a renewed commitment to the provision of welfare for citizens in the twenty-first century. It is based upon the   assumption that welfare is a common good and that it is the role of societies to seek to meet the common good. As social beings we all have a shared interest, and investment, in the relations that we have with our fellow citizens and the interdependencies that these produce. As Defoe's famous novel sought to reveal, even the mythical Robinson Crusoe could not survive on his island without social support.

Our welfare is therefore dependent upon our relations with our fellow citizens. Although, as I shall explain, these relations and this dependency can, in practice, become complex and challenging. What is more, this requires us to engage in and to support collective actions to meet our shared welfare needs and to promote the common good. Despite the powerful impact of some recent ideological discourses about the freedom and responsibility we have as individuals, a moment's reflection reveals that what we can secure for ourselves as individuals is very limited, and in practice is always dependent upon cooperation and collaboration with others. We might want to decide as individuals which newspapers and books we read, what clothes we buy and even what pension investments we make, but someone else has written and published those books, and designed and made those clothes, and decided on the costs and benefits of the different (and sometimes fairly limited) pension schemes on offer.

We also depend on others to meet our needs for welfare. The provision of welfare is intrinsically and inevitably a collective, not an individual, matter. The important questions, therefore, are what do we mean by, or understand by, welfare, and what forms of collective action are best able to deliver it? In practice these can sometimes be complex, even apparently contradictory, problems, and the answers to them are not always simple ones, as I will aim to explain. However, they do all come down to different forms of collective action, within different organisational platforms and aimed at different aspects of our social lives. We need to decide what we want from these forms and how best to work together to realise them effectively. This is a normative debate, based upon the values that we aspire to as well as the practical obstacles that we face in achieving these.

Welfare

Welfare itself is an ambiguous term – or rather it has been used ambiguously by politicians, policy makers and academics. Thus, although it is at the heart of debates about how and why we should provide support to our fellow citizens, it has become a contested concept. On the one hand, welfare is clearly a good thing. Sometimes linked to the related notion of wellbeing, it has been used by the supporters of social action to meet human needs. Thus, welfare and wellbeing are the positive outcomes of the actions we take to protect and support citizens, and the services we provide to meet individual needs so that they can lead healthy and fulfilling lives (an issue explored further in Chapter 2). Quite what this means in terms of practical action, however, soon becomes rather more complex.

Welfare has also come to be associated with the receipt of support from these public actions, and indeed our reliance on this, as opposed to independence and self-sufficiency. Here the connotation is a negative one of welfare dependency, something which we might fear and wish to discourage. This usage has also become more common in the UK in recent times, with 'welfare' sometimes used to refer to receipt of (or indeed dependency upon) social security benefits, especially means-tested ones, which is how welfare is also generally perceived in the USA.

Despite these contradictory connotations, however, it is the notion of welfare as the positive objective for social action that underpins the arguments developed in this book. This includes explanation of the development of the 'welfare state', as the organised national framework for policy actions to meet social needs, and discussion of some of the 'welfare services' which have been provided to deliver these. As I shall explain in Chapter 4, despite the development of the welfare state, not all welfare services are in fact delivered by public agencies. In all welfare regimes many are provided by commercial or third sector (voluntary) agencies, and the scope of these has been increasing in the UK and elsewhere in recent times.

The focus of this book, therefore, is on the provision of welfare in modern society, and why we need to promote and protect this. For the most part I will be discussing welfare provision in the UK. However, in practice many of the key features of UK welfare provision, and the challenges to this, are similar to those found in most other developed industrial countries, so in places I will draw on comparative examples from other countries – most notably those in the Organisation for Economic Co-operation and Development (OECD), which collects information about policies and outcomes across its member nations.

Academic discussion of welfare provision largely focuses on the role of social policy in delivering this. Students of social policy, as an academic subject, study the planning and delivery of welfare services, and social policy is part of a broader 'public policy', which also includes things like transport and environmental planning. These are important aspects of our collective investment and common good, but I shall focus mainly on social policy and the provision of welfare. So this book is also about why we need social policy, and what some of the key issues informing the academic study of social policy are.

The welfare state

The collective provision of welfare services has a long history. In the UK this history can be traced back at least to the Poor Laws of Elizabethan England, first introduced in 1601, which gave discretionary local support to people who were then described as vagrants. It was in the nineteenth century, however, when more widespread public measures were introduced to meet a number of the welfare needs of a wider range of people in society. These included education in primary schools, vaccination and sanitation to promote public health, and the growth of both public and private hospitals. Not all of these early welfare services were publicly provided. Hospitals and schools were often privately founded by individuals or voluntary organisations, in particular, churches, which ran a number of the early primary schools. Local Poor Law Relief was also supplemented, or replaced, by insurance payments to unemployed workers from Friendly Societies, which collected subscriptions from members to fund support at times of need. And in the latter part of the century a national body, the Charity Organisation Society (COS), was setup to coordinate and promote the voluntary provision of welfare services.

The role of the COS in the promotion of charitable welfare provision came under particular scrutiny in the deliberations of the Royal Commission on the Poor Laws, established to make recommendations for the future development of welfare support at the beginning of the twentieth century. Some leading COS figures were members of the Commission and were largely behind the *Majority Report*, which was published in 1909 and argued that charitable provision should continue to play a central role in future development of welfare in the UK. However, these views were challenged by a *Minority Report*, which was largely the work of Beatrice Webb. She and her husband Sidney were leading members of the Fabian Society, which had been set up at the end of the nineteenth century to campaign for the public provision of welfare through the state, and this is just what the *Minority Report* argued for.

Importantly, the two reports represented rather different visions of how we should develop welfare services. One (the *Majority Report*) arguing for non-state providers; and the other (the *Minority Report*) arguing for state welfare. These disagreements ran so deep that no consensus could be reached in a single report. These are differences that continue to influence debates about the development of welfare over a hundred years later, at the beginning of the twenty-first century, with support for privately provided market welfare and voluntary action through third sector organisations included in what has always, in practice, been a *mixed economy* of welfare. However, what was not contested within the Commission was the then need to expand and deepen the collective provision of welfare to meet the needs of a growing population, many of whom were living in or near poverty.

In the early years of the twentieth century welfare services were expanded significantly, under a reforming Liberal government led by Asquith and Lloyd George. These included an expansion of state schools, and the introduction of health insurance, Labour Exchanges, old-age pensions, and unemployment and sickness insurance. Although the insurance provision was modelled on the work of the Friendly Societies, and included them in some aspects of provision, these reforms, and most of the other changes, were based upon commitments to use the state provision and public funding to provide new welfare services. Although theirs was only the *Minority Report*, it was largely the Fabian Society's support for state welfare that carried the day.

The early twentieth-century reforms introduced state welfare to the UK, and these reforms were being repeated in similar forms in most other industrial nations. Indeed, it had been the introduction of unemployment insurance by the German Chancellor Otto von Bismarck in the late nineteenth century, that had provided the

5

model for this across much of the rest of Europe, including the UK. However, it was the more extensive reforms made by the Labour government of Clement Attlee after the end of the Second World War, that transformed public welfare services into the welfare state.

The post-war Labour government is often credited with the creation of a welfare state in Britain, because the extensive new provisions that were introduced were all based on a commitment to the provision of comprehensive welfare services delivered by national government agencies and funded from national taxation. They included a new social security scheme (National Insurance), a major programme of new public housing, compulsory state education up to age 15 (actually introduced in 1944 by the wartime government, but with Labour support), and, perhaps most significantly, the National Health Service (NHS). This state commitment to comprehensive welfare services had been argued for during the war by the *Beveridge Report* of 1942, which had focused primarily on social security reform but had proposed that much wider public provision was needed to rid the country of what Sir William Beveridge called 'five giant evils': ignorance, squalor, idleness, disease and want. In this short and pithy list Beveridge captured much of the case for welfare intervention to meet social needs. And although the words may now seem dated, concern over these social evils still underpins the case for welfare support today.

It was Beveridge's (1942) call for social welfare, together with the arguments of the economist Keynes (1936) that governments should seek to manage national economies to promote economic growth and employment, that created the political and ideological climate for the introduction of the welfare state in the UK. And it was a pattern that was being followed in most other advanced industrial countries in the middle of the last century. However, this proved to be something of a high water mark for public welfare provision. Although the welfare state was widely supported and further developed over the next two to three decades, in the 1970s and 1980s it came under pressure from economic changes and political attacks.

laisser faire

A mixed economy of welfare

Economic recession in the 1970s caused some to raise questions over whether it was possible to continue to fund, and to expand, comprehensive public welfare services for all, particularly if this threatened market-based economic growth. By the 1980s this had affected all advanced welfare regimes (Pierson, 1998). In the UK political change, under the Conservative governments of Margaret Thatcher, also led to questions about the desirability of state welfare for all, particularly as, it was argued, this might crowd out private market alternatives and discourage individual citizens from providing for themselves. This move away from Keynesian policies of state support for public welfare towards a belief that it is only free markets that can best meet the dual goals of economic growth and individual freedom is sometimes referred to as neoliberalism, in part because it implies a call to return to the economic liberalism (or *laissez faire*) of the nineteenth century, before the state began to intervene to respond to social needs and economic pressures – and I will return to discuss the challenge of neoliberalism in more detail in Chapter 7.

Neoliberalism is also associated with the anti-state reforms of the Reagan administrations in the US in the 1980s. (Reagan and Thatcher were close political allies.) But it also began to inform welfare reforms in a number of other countries that had earlier expanded state welfare. This led to cuts in spending plans in many countries (sometimes referred to as welfare *retrenchment*) and to moves to contract out services to private and third sector providers – further accentuating the mixed economy of welfare.

This shift towards a welfare mix could also be found in the politics and policies of the Labour governments in the UK in the 2000s. The Labour government promoted a 'third way' approach, between the state and the market, and championed choice and competition within public welfare services. This was taken much further by the Coalition and Conservative governments of David Cameron, however, who, in response to the economic recession of

2008, also introduced a wide-ranging programme of cuts in welfare expenditure designed to reduce dramatically public borrowing and the deficit that had grown in the public finances. Cameron referred to the government's aim as promoting a 'Big Society', as an alternative to the big state of the post-war welfare regime; and the austerity measures (as they were called) were planned to reduce overall public spending as a proportion of Gross Domestic Product (GDP) from around 47 to 41 per cent, taking it below most comparable OECD nations.

In practice the Coalition government found it difficult to meet the public deficit reduction targets, however, not least because they also sought to protect to some extent some key areas of welfare spending, such as the NHS and education in schools. Nevertheless, the return of a Conservative government in 2015 meant that by the mid-2010s the impact of neoliberalism on the politics of welfare in the UK was clearly established, with public expenditure on welfare the main target for plans to reduce the public sector deficit by cutting spending rather than raising taxation.

In the twentieth century the key factors that underpinned the development of welfare were the Fabian arguments for comprehensive protection through the state and Beveridge's call to use public services to rid the country of social evils; these led to the creation of a welfare state. At the beginning of the twenty-first century support for the welfare state has been challenged by a neoliberal discourse of individual choice and responsibility, and market competition. The key questions that underpin welfare development are now different: critics ask whether we can afford to maintain a welfare state to respond to ever growing and more complex welfare needs, and whether comprehensive public services are not removing individual choice and responsibility from citizens in meeting their welfare needs.

It is the contrast between these two viewpoints, and the ideological and political arguments that lie behind them, that I take up in this book. I want to revisit some of the core arguments for the provision of welfare that lie behind these different perspectives, and some of the different forms that welfare provision can take in responding to these. This is organised and developed around discussion of some of the more practical questions that flow from these broader ideological choices:

- What do we mean by welfare?
- What are the main welfare issues?
- How should we deliver welfare?
- Where should planning and delivery of welfare take place?
- Who should benefit from welfare?
- What social and economic challenges does the provision of welfare face?
- Why do we need a new approach to collective action?

The sociological imagination

I approach these questions as a social scientist. That is, with a commitment to using theoretical analysis and empirical data to make sense of the social relations that shape our societies and our experiences of living in them. Many modern social scientists cite the book *The sociological imagination* by the American author C. Wright Mills as an inspiration to their endeavours to understand social relations.

Wright Mills was Professor of Sociology at Columbia University in New York, and he wrote the book shortly before he died in 1959 (it has subsequently been republished in 2000) at the relatively young age of 45, after a decade in which he had produced a number of influential books on American society, offering a radical challenge to much of the then social science establishment in the US. Wright Mills wanted to promote social science, of which sociology was only one part, because it brought together the private worlds of individuals and the public worlds of social relations. He talked about these as 'personal troubles' and 'public issues', and argued that the job of social scientists was to show how these were, in fact, different sides of the same coin; the means for doing this was the application of the sociological imagination. 'The sociological imagination enables us to grasp history and biography and the relations between the two within society' (Wright Mills, 2000, p 6). It is what social scientists do.

The terms 'personal troubles' and 'public issues' remind us that, for social scientists, our needs and our concerns have both individual and collective dimensions. This is true of welfare needs: poverty is both an individual and a social problem. More generally, though, it underpins the way social scientists understand and analyse social relations, through the interaction of *structure* and *agency*.

Structures are the established social contexts that influence our social relations, from the 'hard' structures of rules and regulations to the 'softer' structures of institutional values and cultures. At the same time, however, individual actors have choices about how (and whether) to act within these structural constraints. And, more generally, these social structures are themselves the products of the cumulative and collective actions all of those operating within them. As Karl Marx pointed out back in 1852, 'Men make their own history, but they do not make it as they please ... but under circumstances ... given and transmitted from the past' (Marx, 1869, p 10). More recently, contemporary understanding of the interaction of structure and agency has been developed by Giddens in what he calls his theory of 'structuration'. It is through the actions of agents and their ensuing social outcomes, he argues, that social structures are created and recreated. Or, as he puts it, 'Society only has form, and that form only has effects on people, in so far as structure is produced and reproduced in what people do' (Giddens and Pierson, 1998, p 77).

The sociological imagination and the theory of structuration teach us that although we are all individuals, we also exist and act within social contexts. Our personal troubles are also public issues, to use Wright Mills' terms, and we need to remember the implications of this when thinking about welfare needs and welfare services. For instance, as discussed in Chapter 3, even though we might have saved into a private pension scheme, we can only spend the money from that on goods and services provided by others, and we will depend on them to secure the value of our savings. To give another example, although we can buy private healthcare and private education from commercial providers, the doctors, nurses and teachers that work for these providers will have been trained and no doubt gained experience in public welfare agencies.

Another central feature of Wright Mills' discussion of the role of the sociological imagination was his commitment to social science as a *normative* enterprise. That is, he believed that social scientists should be seeking to change the world as well as to understand it – or rather, that they should understand the world in order to change it. We should be concerned not only with what *is* but also what *ought to be*. And underpinning this, for Wright Mills and many other social scientists, is a concern to understand, and to promote, the *common good*.

The common good

The idea of the common good, or sometimes just the *commons*, has had a longstanding place in philosophical, political and economic debate about social relations. It is based on recognition of the need to balance individual freedom with social responsibility or, as the American author Sievers (2010) argued, the 'conflict between individual interests and collective needs' (p xv). All societies must balance these potentially contradictory pressures, and this is done by seeking between them the common good. That is, the collective values, practices and outcomes that we all share. For without these, societies cannot survive or flourish.

What is more, as I will return to discuss in Chapter 8, the common good is an enduring, and cumulative, outcome of individual and social actions. In all societies we rely upon the common goods produced and developed through earlier collective actions. These include basic infrastructures like the railway system, welfare institutions like hospitals, trained and skilled individuals like teachers and nurses, and collective investments like Beveridge's

National Insurance scheme. Without common goods like these our society would not function as it does. And, of course, to ensure that it will continue to function we need to continue to invest in the future production of the common good.

It is my belief in the centrality of the common good as the essential security for future successful social relations that underpins the arguments developed in this book to address the questions facing the future development of welfare. Like Wright Mills, I believe that this is fundamentally a normative enterprise. We should understand the common good in order to promote it. And this means understanding and promoting the need for collective action to secure the welfare that we need to maintain the common good. In essence, this is why we need welfare.

However, we need a new approach to the collective provision of welfare in the twenty-first century, based upon a model of collective action that goes beyond the publicly delivered services of the twentieth-century welfare state. What is more, how we respond to this need for welfare is not a simple matter, as those who have studied the social policies developed to deliver it understand only too well. In the following chapters I will seek to do justice to some of this practical complexity, while trying to keep a hold on the core message of the need for collective action for the common good; and in Chapter 8 I will conclude by arguing that we need a new focus for collective action to achieve this.

Key texts

Daly's (2011) introduction to the concept of welfare provides a good summary of the main conceptual debates about this.In the same series, Dean's (2012) book on social policy outlines the key dimensions of the academic study of the subject. Richard Titmuss is generally regarded as the most important academic writer on, and supporter of, state welfare, and a summary of some of his key works can be found in Alcock et al (2001). The best history of the post-war welfare state in the UK is Timmins (2001), which takes its title from Beveridge's evils. Castles (1999 and 2004) has developed comparative analyses of the changes to welfare provision across advanced industrial societies, and has examined the evidence for and against the impact of retrenchment. Wright Mills (2000) remains for me the most inspiring book on the importance of social science. Though it is over 50 years old, its core messages still resonate with the challenges we face in understanding twenty-first-century society.

2

What do we mean by welfare?

At the heart of the issues that I want to address in this book is the dual nature of welfare as both an individual concern and a collective good. We need welfare to respond to what Wright Mills (2000) called private troubles and public issues, and it is the dual character of this challenge, and the ways in which we respond to it, that determines what we mean by welfare in practice. The purpose of this chapter is to explore some of the major questions underpinning the organisation and delivery of welfare services. What are we seeking to achieve? And why does this matter? I will examine these questions and the problems flowing from them that welfare provision needs to address; and the practical and political challenges that these pose for its development and delivery.

Individual needs and social problems

Individual needs and social problems are challenges to any society and require us to respond to them. But they are not necessarily the same, and they may require different forms of response. Needs, we experience as individuals, though not all individuals would agree on what we need. In this context we can make a simple distinction between needs and wants: we may *want* to have rhinoplasty to reshape our nose, but we *need* to have surgery to set our broken leg. More generally, of course, we may want all sorts of things, but welfare is about the collective response to the needs that we all, to some extent, share.

However, even agreeing on what we need is far from simple and, indeed, may be contested. In a widely quoted analysis, Bradshaw (1972) sought to get around this potential contestation by developing what he called a 'taxonomy of needs', which distinguished between:

- normative need – based on need as norm or standard, usually set by experts, such as the level of social security benefits or nutritional standards in diets;
- felt need – based on individual perceptions, what people think they really need;
- expressed need – based on what people say they need and act to secure; for instance, waiting lists for hospital operations are an expression of the need for hospital treatments;
- comparative need – which emerges by comparison with others who are not in need; if some people in particular circumstances are not receiving services that others in the same position are, then they may be in need of these.

The taxonomy of needs includes, in the concept of expressed need, what economists sometimes refer to as *preferences*, arguing that we can only really know what people think are needs by looking at their behaviour and whether they seek things or express a demand for them. This provides us with a measurable definition, which economists like, but it overlooks those things that we may not understand or know that we need – this is why we carry out screening for cancers, for example. It also ignores much comparative need, because we may not know what others have that we might be missing.

Because of these uncertainties and disagreements, some people have argued that needs are essentially *relative* phenomena – that is, different people will have different needs in different (or even the same) circumstances. However, some proponents of welfare have argued that this is not the case, and that we can (and should) aim to identify (and then to meet) *absolute* needs. In their book *Human need*, Doyal and Gough argued that we could identify two absolute human needs, which would apply to 'everyone, everywhere' (1991, p 59). These were health and autonomy, because we all need to be as healthy as we can be and we all need to be able to act as effective social beings.

A similar logic lies behind the work of Amartya Sen (2009), who has developed the argument that all people have a right to be capable of having the freedom to live the kind of life that they want to lead – sometimes referred to as the 'capability approach'. As with Doyal and Gough's autonomy, for Sen, capability is a basic human need, and it has been widely taken up in debates about poverty and social exclusion in particular. More recently, it has been further developed by Nussbaum (2011) in her argument that we should be 'creating capabilities' for human development to meet our most basic human needs for dignity and self-respect.

For these authors, human needs are individual needs, but they require a response from society. Health and autonomy can only be realised if social services and legal frameworks are developed to support these. Individual needs are also linked to social problems, however. For instance, one of the first social policy responses to the need for individual health was to use programmes of public vaccination to combat the spread of contagious diseases. Contagious diseases are a social problem – indeed, potentially a global problem, as the Ebola crisis of 2014/15 graphically demonstrated. Vaccination not only protects individuals but prevents diseases spreading across society – and beyond.

In practice, however, social problems are, as the term implies, socially defined. Individuals may feel their own needs, but social problems only exist if they threaten the social order. Within social discourse, therefore, the nature of social problems is contentious. For instance, what we mean by the problem of homelessness is much debated. Is it restricted literally to sleeping rough, or does it extend to people living in overcrowded dwellings? (And what constitutes overcrowding?) How we define a problem like homelessness has consequences for the social responses that we expect to make to it – to relieve overcrowding we are going to need to build a lot more new houses.

Debate about the nature and extent of social problems is thus a clear example of normative discussion of the need for welfare. As with individual needs, how we identify social problems is a subject of political and policy debate. The housing charity Shelter, for example, has been active for around 50 years in presenting evidence about the extent of the problem of homelessness and arguing for particular policy responses to this. They can rightly claim to have made a major contribution to putting homelessness onto the social policy 'map', although they would be the first to admit that this has not brought an end to the problem, and that more needs to be done to persuade us of the need for further concerted collective action.

Discussions of individual needs and social problems are therefore inextricably interlinked. Indeed, in a sense they are perhaps merely different dimensions of the same phenomenon: the failing of society to promote the welfare of all of its citizens.

Welfare and wellbeing

In Chapter 1 I linked the concept of welfare to that of wellbeing, arguing that both have been used to describe the objectives of social policy, and indeed this is the case. However, arguably, in practice they are not interchangeable terms. When explored in more detail they reveal two rather different understandings of individual needs and social problems, and the responses to these.

Despite the negative connotations associated with welfare as referring to means-tested social security benefits, welfare has generally been used to describe the objective of meeting people's broader needs for social security. Our welfare determines our place in society and underpins our ability to participate successfully in social relations. In this sense, welfare is very much a collective good.

By contrast, wellbeing has more often been used to describe individual happiness and flourishing. There is much debate about what we mean by happiness and flourishing, for instance, the positive psychology ideas discussed by Seligman (2011). There is survey research that seeks to identify whether people are happy and why they think this is, and there is philosophical debate, which can be traced back to Aristotle, about what might be the key characteristics of human flourishing. These do have a social dimension, of course, but wellbeing is often used more restrictively (especially by economists) to refer to how we feel and how we behave as individuals. The concern with wellbeing is therefore a concern more with our feelings and behaviour.

This more individualistic focus also leads to rather different forms of policy interventions to promote wellbeing than the collective public services that have been developed to meet our need for welfare. Policies to promote wellbeing seek to influence our feelings and our behaviour. This can be seen clearly in policies aimed at shaping our individual health – for instance, banning or discouraging smoking, promoting balanced diets, or exhorting us to take more exercise. If we follow this advice and change our lifestyle, we should be healthier and so improve our wellbeing. And policies to encourage – or to *nudge* – us to change our lifestyles are at the centre of a number of recent initiatives to improve wellbeing in the UK.

The idea of using incentives and sanctions to 'nudge' people into changing their behaviour, and hence improving their lifestyle, has been popularised by an American economist and lawyer, Thaler and Sunstein (2008). More recently, it became the focus of the work of a special Behavioural Insights Team within the UK Cabinet Office, whose job was to encourage other government departments to take up such indirect policy initiatives to bring about changes in people's lives. Quite how successful such policy nudges are in practice is still much disputed. Clearly few would doubt that giving up smoking or improving diet are likely to improve individual health and life outcomes, but such individual behavioural changes are unlikely to be effective independently of other collective social policy interventions, such as regulations to ban smoking in public places or to set nutritional standards for foodstuffs.

Even this promotion of individual wellbeing has a broader social context. Restrictions on smoking benefit us all in providing a cleaner environment and reducing the cost of medical treatment for smoking-related illnesses. So wellbeing is never just an individual behavioural issue. Yet the tendency for wellbeing to refer more narrowly to individual lifestyle and behavioural changes, means that it can lead us to underestimate the need for collective policy responses to secure for all citizens a healthy and active place in society. Thus both welfare and wellbeing are normative terms, and I argue that both should be used to inform social debate and policy action.

Social justice

Arguments for welfare are based on the response to needs and problems, and this includes both collective action to promote welfare and individual actions to secure wellbeing. To some extent, this is a practical, or a political, response to felt needs, or expressed demands. However, the case for welfare is also based on moral arguments about the desirability of welfare, and these are often linked to arguments for social justice. We respond to people's needs and problems because we think that it is right, or fair, to do so.

More generally, the case for the development of a welfare state is linked to the case for a more just society – and in this sense, therefore, it is also linked to arguments for social change. In part, this is about equality and inequality; it is no coincidence that the impact of many of the policy reforms associated with the creation of the welfare state has been to reduce the levels of inequality that would have existed in society without them. The moral question that lies behind this, therefore, is whether we can have a just or fair society where some people have very much more than more others, and where some have so little that they are struggling to meet their basic needs and provide for themselves and their families.

I have used the terms 'just' and 'fair' to describe this moral concern. However, justice and fairness are not necessarily interchangeable concepts – and certainly are often used differently in political and policy discourses about welfare. Here, the difference could be summarised rather simplistically as meaning that justice is where you get what you need and fairness is where you get what you deserve, although common usage of the two terms does not always stick very closely to this distinction.

Getting what you need is linked to the role of welfare in meeting individual and social needs, as discussed above, and the case for social justice is a case for collective social action to achieve this. In the early 1990s the then leader of the UK Labour Party, John Smith, set up a Commission on Social Justice under the chairmanship of Lord Borrie (1994) to examine the arguments for different forms of collective action to meet social needs. This provided the ideological framework for many of the welfare reforms later introduced by the Labour governments of 1997 to 2010, which included some significant expansion of public expenditure on welfare services such as education and health.

Getting what you deserve is linked to a more individual notion of entitlement or rights to welfare, based on what people have contributed to society and can therefore expect back in return. This more individualistic notion of fairness has been taken up most recently by the UK government in its arguments that fairness is based upon responsibility, and that it is not fair that people who have not contributed to society (by working and paying taxes) should be able to benefit from it – the alleged 'something for nothing society' of welfare dependency.

This narrower notion of fairness as based upon reward clearly does appeal to some popular ideas about entitlement and rights. However, it is not associated only with the welfare dependency concerns of the UK government. Indeed, the model behind the social insurance benefits to provide for pensions and unemployment benefits introduced by Bismarck in Germany in the nineteenth century, and promoted by Beveridge in his arguments for the National Insurance (NI) scheme introduced in Britain by the post-war Attlee government, was based upon entitlement to social security support at times of unemployment, in return for contributions into the scheme made while in employment. Under such social insurance schemes, people are only entitled to benefits if they have made sufficient contributions into the scheme – a rather strict notion of fairness, which it is nevertheless argued has continually attracted significant popular support for these insurance schemes.

The notion of entitlement, or rights to welfare, as the basis for social support was developed further by T.H. Marshall (1950) at about the same time as the post-war welfare state reforms were introduced in the UK. Marshall argued that it was possible to identify different kinds of rights, which were also associated with the development of more extensive public responsibilities through the state. These were:

- property rights, the first, associated with ownership and the growth of capitalism;
- civil rights, such as the right to vote, associated with the growth of democracy;
- social rights, the most recent, associated with the twentieth-century welfare state.

Social rights provided a more extensive notion of citizenship, in effect, giving citizens a right to call on the collective resources of the state, in return for contributions to these collective resources through taxes and insurance contributions. This notion of all contributing to and being entitled to social rights has been a critically important feature of the organisation of the public welfare provision in the UK and in other advanced industrial countries, as I describe in the later chapters of this book.

Marshall's social rights are also linked to broader arguments about the nature, and the desirability, of social justice. We believe in social justice because we recognise that social rights are dependent upon collective commitments to provide for all – and we all have an interest in benefiting from this. One of the most widely quoted attempts to explain, and justify, social justice is that set out by the American philosopher John Rawls in his 1971 book *A theory of justice* (1999). Rawls argued that our notion of social justice should be informed by an objective assessment of the amount of difference (or the extent of need) that we could expect to tolerate in society, and that this could be determined by asking people what distribution of resources they would consider just if they did not know what position they would occupy within this distribution. This would take self-interest (or self-preservation) out of the equation and lead to minimum standards that should guarantee to protect the least well-off. From this he developed two principles of social justice – see Box 2.1.

Box 2.1 Rawls' principles of justice

First, each person is to have an equal right to the most extensive basic liberty compatible with a similar liberty for others.

Second, social and economic inequalities are to be arranged so that they are both (a) to the greatest benefit to the least advantaged and (b) attached to offices and positions open to all under conditions of fair equality of opportunity. (Rawls, 1999, p 71).

For Rawls, therefore, social justice was related to equality, as discussed below, including equality of opportunity – the possibility of occupying different positions in the social order. Here too, there are links to Sen and Nussbaum's notions of capability. In order to take advantage of opportunities, we need to be able to realise our potential and have the freedom and capability to participate in society.

Arguments for social justice, therefore, are arguments for social rights, and for the role of public supports and services to deliver these. They are also arguments for a more equal and acceptable social order, and for ensuring that all citizens have the freedom and the capacity to participate in this. Social justice is thus about collective action and participation in society, and, as I shall return to in Chapter 8, it is therefore also predicated upon our pursuit of the common good.

These are rather theoretical, or philosophical, arguments for social justice, however, and indeed much of the debate about the principles of justice, rights and fairness has been conducted by philosophers. They do not tell us what social justice means in practice – that is, how much inequality is acceptable, what social rights should be guaranteed or what responsibilities states and citizens should have. There are, of course, no correct, or agreed, answers to these questions, and we will all have different ideas about what these should be – including me. The important point is that it is normative debate about the answers to these questions that ought to be at the centre of discourses on social justice.

The study of social policy provides a space for debate to be developed about what we think should be the forms and outcomes of social relations, and why we think these are important. Arguments for social justice are at the heart of the case for why we need welfare. For the most part, however, these arguments take place within the boundaries of national welfare states. There is also the wider issue of what we might call 'global social justice', and the extent to which the discourses of equality, rights and fairness should be extended onto a comparative global scale. Here the practical implications quickly become much more challenging, of course, because the world is a profoundly unequal place with billions denied even many basic rights – and denied civil and property rights, as well as social ones. This is a challenge that is beyond the scope of this book, which focuses on the UK welfare state and similar regimes in other developed OECD nations – although we do need to address the issues of global social justice too, not least because these increasingly impact on us all.

Equality and inequality

The problem of inequality is at the centre of the case for social justice. As Rawls argues, social justice is driven by the amount of inequality, or the levels of equality, we are prepared to tolerate in society. Too much inequality is unjust. What is more, actions to reduce inequality have been the most important elements of policy interventions to promote welfare. The redistribution of resources and the provision of minimum standards for all are the most common aims, and outcomes, of welfare services. Equality and inequality are central to both the theoretical case for welfare and the practical actions taken to achieve it.

To look at this another way: inequality is a problem for welfare, as has been recognised since the early days of state welfare in the UK and elsewhere. In 1913 in an early lecture on 'Poverty as an industrial problem', the Christian socialist and historian R.H. Tawney put this rather sharply: 'What thoughtful rich people call the problem of poverty, thoughtful poor people call with equal justice a problem of riches' (p 10).

All societies are unequal to some extent, but the scale of these inequalities matters. And if some people do not have enough to survive or participate in society (a point discussed in Chapter 3), it is most likely because some others have much more than they need. The scale of the gap between those at the bottom and those at the top can mean that rich and poor people within the same society can feel as though they are living, both economically and culturally, in different worlds. Indeed, it is likely that neither group will have very much idea about how the other lives, so they are not even able to compare their lots in the way that Rawls' notion of social justice might presume. Evidence suggests that rich people often overestimate the incomes and resources of the poor, and that poorer people often significantly underestimate the scale of the wealth enjoyed by those at the top. In a classic study of perceptions of inequality published in 1966, Runciman argued that in practice people tended to compare their 'relative deprivation' with those quite close to them in the social hierarchy rather than those at the other end of the wealth spectrum.

Social scientists often use statistical measures to examine levels of inequality in society. At a very broad level, the extent of inequality within a society can be represented by the Gini coefficient, a decimal measure between 0 and 1, which is higher where inequality is greater. This can be used to compare the levels of inequality between different societies or within one society over time. Figure 2.1 tracks the Gini coefficient in the UK since 1977. It reveals how it rose significantly in the 1980s and has remained broadly stable since then – with no return to the greater equality found in the earlier period.

Figure 2.1 Gini coefficients, 1997 to 2012/13

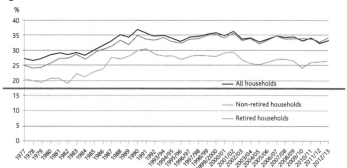

Source: Office for National Statistics (2014, p 19)

What this broad measure does not reveal, however, is the spread of inequality across the population, particularly the high concentration of income and wealth at the top end. This can be seen in figures that break the population down into different groups and compare their incomes with each other and against the average. This pictorial representation was pioneered by Pen, and has been used by Hills (2015) in his recent detailed analysis of inequality and welfare in the UK. Figure 2.2 is taken from Hills and reveals, as Pen initially pointed out, that most of the population have incomes far below the average, and that this is because those at the top have incomes very much higher than this.

In fact, even this picture does not disclose the massive gap in incomes between those at the very top and the rest of the population. People within the top 1 per cent of the population in the UK, and some other countries like the US, have incomes way beyond the distribution captured in a graph like the one shown

Figure 2.2 Pen's parade of incomes in the UK, 2010/11

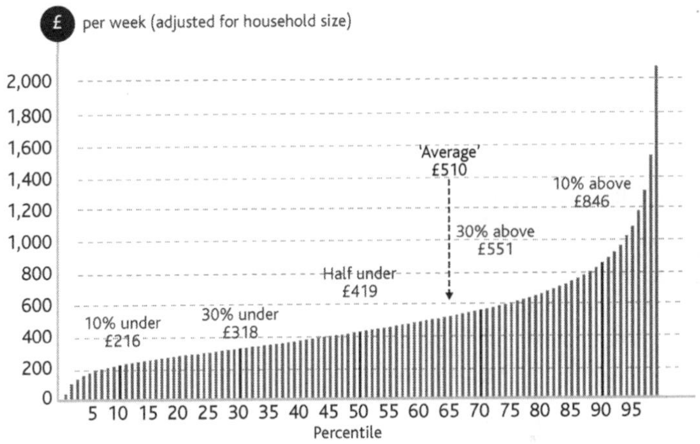

Source: Hills (2015), Figure 2.5

in Figure 2.2. This is because there are people like professional footballers on incomes of £200,000 a week and top bankers with annual incomes (topped up by bonuses) of many millions of pounds a year. What is more, this only represents income inequality. When we also take account of holdings of capital and other forms of wealth (such as property), then the gap between the top 1 per cent and the rest becomes even greater. Andrew Sayer (2014) has explored the extent of the income and wealth holdings of the rich in UK and US society, along with the dysfunctional consequences of this for the rest of the population, and indeed the economy more generally, in his book *Why we can't afford the rich*. Similar arguments have also been developed by the French social scientist, Thomas Piketty (2014), who has tracked economic data over two centuries to compare the recent the rise in inequality. From this, he has argued that it is a trend that will not be reversed by economic markets alone, and which will require government intervention to redistribute resources.

For Sayer and Piketty, the extremes of inequality are both a moral problem and an economic problem for modern societies –

evidence of the continuing importance of Wright Mills' description of social science as a normative enterprise. The economic costs of inequality have been researched in more detail by Wilkinson and Pickett (2009), who have used comparative analysis to show that greater inequality within societies is associated with higher levels of health and other social problems – captured in the title of their book *The spirit level: Why more equal societies almost always do better*. The weight of evidence that inequality is problematic in practice, as well as in principle, is therefore increasingly strong, yet levels of inequality, especially at the top, continue to increase.

Redistribution can be used to correct such inequality – for example, through higher tax rates on high incomes and property holdings – and measures such as these are debated in political discourse in the UK and elsewhere. However, high taxes are only effective in reducing inequality and redistributing resources if they can be collected effectively, and as Sayer (2014) and others have argued, this is made more difficult by the use of overseas tax havens and other tax avoidance measures to hide income and wealth from governments. More generally, redistribution is a means of responding to inequality *post hoc*, taking for granted the massive disparities in incomes and wealth which already exist.

In a recent study of inequality in the UK and the US, Atkinson (2015), who is one of the leading UK economists working in the field, argued that we can only reduce overall levels of inequality by taking account of the broader social and economic factors that have produced it. This means tackling too the 'predistribution' of resources, through more general regulations and controls on income levels and wealth holding. This includes increasing the minimum wages which were introduced in the UK at the end of the last century and are to be extended by the introduction of the Conservatives' so-called living wage between 2016 and 2020. It could be taken much further, too, by restrictions on higher wages and rewards, or even, as Atkinson (2015, p 131) argues, through the introduction of a code of practice for pay and rewards, led by the creation of a 'Social and Economic Council'.

As Atkinson (2015) and others have argued, we can, and should, act collectively to reduce current levels of inequality. And, as Wilkinson and Pickett's (2009) evidence suggests, this will lead to improvements in welfare more generally in society. These are arguments for promoting equality of outcome; they are sometimes contrasted with a different approach based on equality of opportunity – see Box 2.2.

Box 2.2 Equality of opportunity and equality of outcome

Equality of opportunity is based on the belief that all should have an equal chance to reach any status in society. We should all be able to enter the 'race to the top' and have an equal chance of winning it. As it has sometimes been put in America: anyone can become President of the USA (although of course not all can win the race, and only very few make it to become President). Equality of opportunity is linked to discussion of social mobility and the extent to which people can move up (and down) the social hierarchy. If there is much social mobility, then the extent of inequality may not matter so much as, in quasi-Rawlsian terms, anyone can occupy any position. However, people do not enter the race for social position from equal starting points, and there is considerable evidence that in modern UK society the extent of social mobility is very limited, with those starting life at the bottom of the social order more likely to end up there, and those at the top more likely to stay there too (see Hills, 2015, Ch 7).

Equality of outcome is based on the belief that policy interventions should be made to reduce levels of inequality in society, so that the gap between the opportunities available to people is not so great. Although it is sometimes confused with egalitarianism, equality of outcome does not, for most proponents, mean seeking to make all outcomes the same. Rather, the aim is to reduce the extent of inequality in social outcomes, as Atkinson (2015), for example, has argued. And, of course, it may be that more equal outcomes also help to promote social mobility by ensuring that the race to the top is conducted on more of a 'level playing field'.

In his overview of the concept of equality, White (2007) developed a more extensive classification of different forms of equality. He distinguished between five categories:

- Legal equality – all should have the same legal rights, with no one 'above the law'.
- Political equality – all should have democratic rights and be able to participate to some extent in decision making.
- Social equality – all should be included in social relations, with no cultural or physical barriers between people or social groups.
- Economic equality – all should have access to property and resources, although levels of ownership of resources are contested, as discussed above.
- Moral equality – all should be treated or respected as equals, at least formally, and should have the right to assert their claims and to criticise others.

The last of these, moral equality, reminds us that equality is linked to social justice and social rights. The moral treatment of all individuals as equal members of society requires us to respect their social rights and to promote a model of social justice that includes all – in Rawlsian terms, a model that all should find acceptable. Normative debate about the desirability and extent of inequality should be a central part of this. We should be concerned with how much, and how little, people at the extremes of our social order have; how socially just this distribution of resources is; and what collective policy action should be taken to address it. As discussed again in Chapter 3, in Tawney's terms, the problem of poverty is a problem of riches too.

Summary
We need welfare provision to respond to our individual needs and to the social problems that failure to address these can cause. Within this, the collective provision of welfare can be contrasted with a more individualised focus on wellbeing. Recent policy initiatives

have focused on promoting our wellbeing by seeking to influence our individual behaviour, but this also has a wider social context and impact. Underpinning our practical concern for welfare and wellbeing are moral concerns about social justice, and welfare policy should seek to promote social justice in order to ensure that all can participate effectively in society. This means tackling too the problem of inequality, by measures to redistribute resources and reduce initial disparities in income and wealth. We should also be concerned about equality of opportunity, although this too is best addressed by reducing the initial inequalities that prevent some people from realising their full potential in society.

Key texts
As mentioned in Chapter 1, Daly's (2011) introduction to welfare remains a good guide to the key conceptual issues underpinning our understanding of this. Amartya Sen's (2009) book is the best discussion of the capability approach, which has become influential in recent debates about the core aims of welfare policy, and Nussbaum's (2011) development of this is also worth reading. Brighouse (2004) provides a good guide to theories of justice, including Rawls' (1999) influential treatise on social justice. In the same series, White (2007) summarises arguments about equality. Atkinson's (2015) recent book on inequality builds on his earlier work in the field to provide evidence of why this is a problem and to outline the case for policy actions to reduce it.

3

What are the main welfare issues?

What we include within the provision of welfare depends to some extent on how far we extend our understanding of our individual needs and social problems. The scope of welfare also varies in official measures (what should we include in public spending on welfare?), in academic debates (what is covered in the study of social policy?) and in the popular perceptions captured in attitude surveys. The coverage in this chapter is therefore something of a compromise. Most measures of public expenditure on welfare, notably those used by the OECD for international comparison, include spending on health, education and social security (or welfare) benefits. These are also the categories included in surveys of public opinion on welfare, like the British Social Attitudes Surveys I discuss in Chapter 7. I will explore these key issues, and the main policy responses to them in the UK, in this chapter. This means that I do not discuss some other potential welfare issues, such as housing and homelessness, crime and disorder, or family policy and child protection, although these and other issues are covered in most of the more traditional social policy texts.

Poverty, social exclusion and social security

Significant levels of inequality is both a moral and practical problem for societies; this is particularly true of the extreme elements of this inequality. Extreme levels of wealth are a problem at the top, as Sayer (2014) has argued. So, too, is poverty at the bottom. In practice, it has been poverty that has more generally been the focus of debate about the need for welfare and the role of social policy in responding to this. Poverty is a long-established focus for welfare policy, and it is definitely the case that poverty is a problem. Poverty is a normative, not a neutral, term, and debate about poverty is also debate about what is to be done to combat it. As explained in my earlier text on *Understanding poverty* (Alcock, 2006), academic and policy discourses on poverty all anticipate, and promote, policy action.

What is more, policy responses to the problem of poverty have a long-established history. The first Poor Laws were introduced in England in 1601, during the reign of Elizabeth I, and a changing landscape of policy interventions can be charted over the four centuries since then. However, recent academic and policy discourse about poverty really dates from the end of the nineteenth century and the beginning of the twentieth. This was in part driven by research which first discovered evidence of the problem of poverty in the UK, based on the work of Charles Booth (1889) in London and Seebohm Rowntree (1901) in York. Booth and Rowntree both found evidence of significant levels of poverty, in Booth's case, in the capital city of the then British Empire. This was a potentially damning indictment of the supposed economic success of the empire, and, as Booth and Rowntree intended, it led to calls from academics like Tawney, mentioned in Chapter 2, and campaigners like the Fabian Society, for something to be done in response.

Something was done, and in the UK in the early decades of the twentieth century, welfare reforms to introduce old-age pensions and unemployment benefits provided early forms of social security support for those unable to provide for themselves and at risk of poverty. Following the Second World War this social security protection was extended by the National Insurance and National Assistance reforms inspired by the Beveridge Report of 1942, which provided the basis for comprehensive social security benefit support to combat what Beveridge had called 'want'. However, later researchers have argued that this state welfare provision has not succeeded in eradicating poverty, and there has been continued political and policy debate about the problem of poverty, often based on competing notions of what this problem is.

There are some key conceptual distinctions, which help to explain why definitions and policy interventions have remained unresolved. The policy changes of the twentieth century were, in part, an attempt to move from the Poor Law focus on the *relief* of poverty to a social security policy framework aimed at poverty *prevention* – see Box 3.1.

Box 3.1 Poverty relief and poverty prevention

Poverty relief is a response to the *symptoms* of poverty. It is based on the provision of resources to those who are poor in order to relieve their suffering. It was the rationale behind the Poor Laws, and has continued in what commentators call *social assistance* benefits today. These benefits are paid to those outside the labour market, and for the unemployed of working age are fixed at levels below the wages that workers might expect to receive in employment. This has been referred to as the principle of 'less eligibility': the living conditions of the recipients of poverty relief should be worse than those of the lowest paid, as a deterrent to claiming benefits.

Poverty prevention is an attempt to tackle the *causes* of poverty. It is based on the provision of resources to those at risk of poverty because of their social circumstances, for example, unemployment, sickness or retirement from work. These have often been provided through *social insurance* benefits, paid in return for contributions made, as promoted by Bismarck and Beveridge. They are intended to provide social security and are not dependent upon a means-test, although in the UK they have also generally been kept at minimal levels, and for some claimants (for instance those with dependent families) they have not prevented poverty, and have left people having to depend on means-tested social assistance as well.

In practice, therefore, if not in principle, the distinction between poverty relief and poverty prevention, and its implications for social security protection, has not been clear-cut in welfare policy. The picture is further complicated, however, by the contested nature of the problem itself, and the fact that, as mentioned, what we mean by 'poverty' to some extent determines what we do about it. Here, too, there is a difference between two ways of understanding what it means to be poor: *absolute* poverty and *relative* poverty – see Box 3.2.

Box 3.2 Absolute and relative poverty

Absolute poverty is the idea that being in poverty means being without the essentials of life, and it is sometimes referred to as subsistence poverty. It is associated with the work of Booth and Rowntree, who were concerned to identify a subsistence level based on the cost of necessities and then to measure the numbers of people with household incomes below this level, and therefore unable to provide for themselves and their families. Absolute poverty should give us a timeless measure of acute need; in practice, however, what is essential for life varies according to where and when one is living. The subsistence needs identified by Booth and Rowntree at the end of nineteenth century are not really a valid basis for determining what it means to be poor over a hundred years later.

Relative poverty takes up this notion of changes in the nature of poverty over time and place. It has been associated in particular with the work of Peter Townsend (1979), who in the 1950s and 1960s argued that poverty could not be fixed at one subsistence level and that, as overall living standards rose over time, so too should our understanding of what it means to be poor – called at the time a 'rediscovery of poverty'. Thus what we mean by poverty will be relative to the average standard of living of all within society, perhaps as measured by average income levels.

Absolute and relative definitions of poverty result in very different measures of the numbers of people who are poor in society, and also they imply rather different policy responses – although both have their problems. Absolute poverty is addressed by giving people enough to live on, but it is not clear what this might mean in practice. Do I need access to electricity to survive in twenty-first-century Britain, and does this extend to access to the internet too? Conversely, relative poverty is often measured by reference to average incomes. This is potentially a circular approach, suggesting that even if all incomes rise a fixed proportion of people will always be poor. This was ridiculed by the Conservative Cabinet member John Moore in 1989 as a perverse outcome of rising affluence, and taken up again by another Conservative, Iain Duncan Smith, in 2015, who pointed out that reductions in average family incomes could also appear to lead to a reduction in child poverty.

There is an old saying that the 'poor will always be with us', but this should not be taken to mean that relative measures of poverty are necessarily totally contradictory. Relative poverty is to some extent a measure of the degree of inequality: the gap between those at the bottom and those above them, and the numbers who fall below a fixed point in distribution of resources. More pertinently perhaps, it is a measure of how much we are concerned about the extent of the gap and the numbers affected.

The UK government provides regular data on these and other factors in its Households Below Average Income (HBAI) figures. These generally use the level of 60 per cent of median average income (the midpoint in the income distribution) as a proxy measure of poverty, and they calculate this for households both before and after taking account of their housing costs, as these are generally a significant proportion of costs over which households have little control. In 2013/14 the median income after taking account of housing costs was £386 a week; 60 per cent of this was £231 a week, which gives us some idea of what is meant by relative poverty here and how limiting this is. On the figures from 2013/14, 9.6 million households (15 per cent) were poor before taking account of housing costs and 13.2 million (21 per cent) after this. For children the picture was even gloomier, with 2.3 million (17 per cent) poor before housing costs and 3.7 million (28 per cent) after. These are high levels of poverty, at least by this income measure, and children are particularly badly affected, with over a quarter in relative poverty.

A relative definition of poverty therefore links the extent and the experience of poverty to the position of people within the broader social order. In this sense, it is part of our wider concerns about social justice and social citizenship, and this has been taken up more recently by those who have sought to develop a more reflective approach to poverty based on the extent to which people are able to participate in society. It was Townsend who pioneered this too, through his argument that, in addition to the idea of relative poverty, we should also recognise the importance of the notion of *relative deprivation*. It is not just low incomes that create problems for people, but also disadvantage in other aspects of living, such as inadequate housing, poor health or disability, damaging working conditions or declining local environment. These all affect people's standard of living, and may prevent them from being fully active members of society. For instance, lack of public transport can trap people in their local area, and dangerous working conditions can lead to poor health and disability.

Townsend's notion of relative deprivation has since been developed further through the argument that what is really going on here is a form of *social exclusion*. That is, those who do not have the resources and the capability to participate in society in the ways that others do, are poor as a result of their social exclusion. It is a concept that was developed initially in continental Europe and promoted by the EU as a focus for European policy action. It extended the focus of analysis and concern beyond those who are the victims of exclusion, to include also the broader structures and practices of social relations which may be excluding them (Room, 1995). In this sense, it is related to Rawlsian notions of social justice and the idea that we should be promoting societies that are concerned with the status of all citizens and which actively seek to include them.

Towards the end of the last century the EU funded a programme of action to combat social exclusion in member nations (see Room et al, 1993; Alcock, 2006, Ch 4); and when they came into power in 1997 the UK Labour government established a Social Exclusion

Unit (SEU) to invest in a series of projects to target resources on improving social relations in local areas with high levels of economic decline and social deprivation.

Social exclusion is a broader concept than poverty; it leads to a more detailed understanding of need and implies a wider range of policy actions to respond to this. However, it raises similar problems of definition and measurement. What does it mean to say that someone is socially excluded? This has been taken up by academic researchers who have attempted to develop an objective definition of poverty and social exclusion and to use this to measure the numbers of people experiencing these. The first attempt at this was for a television series in the 1980s called *Breadline Britain*. The programmes were based on research carried out by Mack and Lansley (1985), who developed a list of indicators of deprivation, the lack of which meant that people could be classed as poor and socially excluded – people experiencing this lack were then interviewed in the television programmes. Since then, there have been three further projects to develop the list of indicators and to track the numbers deprived of them. These more recent surveys have used the views of respondents to establish consensual definitions of what count as an indicators of need, and have only included in the analysis those who are lacking these because they cannot afford to pay for them. They are called the Poverty and Social Exclusion (PSE) surveys, and the most recent was conducted in 2012 and reported in a new book by Mack and Lansley (2015). See Box 3.3.

Box 3.3 Poverty and social exclusion surveys

Over 90 per cent of people agreed on three top indicators of exclusion for adults:

- adequate heating
- a damp-free home
- two meals a day.

And four for children:

- a warm winter coat
- fresh fruits or vegetables once a day
- new, properly fitting shoes
- three meals a day.

There was similar support for more general lifestyle indicators such as visits to family members, leisure activities and (for children) places to study and play.

In 1983 14 per cent of the population were lacking three or more of these basic necessities. By 2012 this had more than doubled to 33 per cent. In 2012 almost 18 million people could not afford adequate housing. Around 14 million could not afford one or more essential household goods. And 4 million children went without two or more items of need – twice the number as in 1999.

See PSE website at www.poverty.ac.uk

The PSE surveys revealed high levels of poverty and social exclusion in modern Britain, and it is of concern that on these measures of lack of basic necessities, the picture has deteriorated over the last decade or so. This is something of a contrast with the trends revealed in the HBAI figures, which showed a decline in relative poverty on the 60 per cent of income figure between 1998 and 2004, and a largely steady state since then up to 2013. The HBAI figures only measure recorded income, however, whereas the PSE surveys explore people's wider standard of living. What both reveal, is that, despite the robust statistical methods used, our understanding of poverty and social exclusion remains both contested and normative.

In simple terms, what we think the problem is determines what we think should be done about it. In the same way, what we are prepared to do about it influences the way in which the problem is defined. For much of the twentieth century the provision of social security benefits was the main response to the problem of poverty. The wider concept of social exclusion changed this, and the EU, and later the UK Labour governments, introduced new measures, like the SEU, to promote locally based interventions to include citizens in a range of social activities.

Labour were also concerned about the problem of child poverty revealed in the HBAI figures, and in 1999 the Prime Minister, Tony Blair, made a formal pledge to eradicate child poverty in the country by 2020 and to halve it by 2010. The introduction of child tax credits to raise the incomes of poor working families was a key measure intended to help meet this, although by 2010 the 50 per cent reduction in child poverty had not been achieved.

After the UK 2010 election, however, the Coalition government abandoned the SEU and the funding targeted on deprived areas to promote social inclusion, and, as part of their broader goals of reducing welfare spending, Child Benefit was frozen and removed from higher earners, tax credits were scaled back, unemployment benefit levels held below inflation and a range of measures introduced to restrict entitlement for working-age claimants. More significantly perhaps, they argued that poverty was not just a product of low income or lack of necessities. It was also, they claimed, caused by inappropriate lifestyle, poor parenting and lack of employment, and these required changes in behaviour rather than redistribution of resources. This was taken further by the Conservatives in 2015, who introduced changes in the definition of child poverty, away from an income measure based on the HBAI to a focus instead on the proportion of children living in workless households and the levels of educational attainment by school pupils, along with other measures based on family breakdown, debt and addiction. Once again, changes in the direction of policy were linked to changing definitions of the problem.

For a government that wanted to reduce public spending, particularly on social security benefits and tax credits, a definition of poverty that focused attention on behaviour change rather than financial support was attractive, and it potentially shifted the debate away from a concentration on statistical analysis of income distribution as the primary measure of policy outcomes. What it also did, of course, was to bring into focus the contrast between the structural and agency dimensions of poverty and social exclusion.

As explained in Chapter 1, all social relations are the product of the interaction of structure and agency; this is also true of poverty and social exclusion. The statistics on income distribution capture the structural impact of economic forces on households. But individuals and households also have choices about how they use their resources, and indeed, how they live their lives. Pioneering research by Oscar Lewis (1965 and 1968) in Puerto Rico in the 1960s explored how families living in poverty developed a 'culture of poverty' to help them cope with deprivation, in particular, suppressing expectations of improving their wealth and living largely 'from day to day'.

The families in Lewis's research learned to survive, rather than to prosper. But it was not just their cultural choices that kept them in poverty. Most did have very low incomes; prospects for employment were poor, and few, if any, could afford to leave their neighbourhoods. Culture was clearly inextricably linked to structure here, as indeed it is for the experience of poverty everywhere. The PSE researchers were concerned to seek to capture this interaction of structure and agency in their research on social exclusion, only including in their calculations those who lacked the consensually agreed indicators if they could not afford to pay for them. Choosing to eat only one meal a day as part of a diet regime was not regarded by the researchers as evidence of the lack of a necessity leading to deprivation or exclusion.

Thus, while we might want to respect the lifestyle choices that people make, and we might want to encourage active parenting and take-up of appropriate employment, we must also recognise that structural factors will limit the scope of agency and the choices that agents make; for those at the bottom of the economic order and living in deprived circumstances, like those in Lewis's (1965 and 1968) studies in Puerto Rico, these choices will be much more constrained. To change these, collective economic and social reform is also needed, and this is just what the PSE researchers, following in the tradition of Booth, Rowntree and Townsend, were seeking to promote.

Research evidence on poverty and social exclusion is used by campaigners to argue the case for policy responses to combat the problem – most notably in the UK in the work of the Child Poverty Action Group (CPAG), established by a group of academics in the 1960s, and still active in leading campaigns for policy reform as well as advising and supporting children and parents experiencing poverty. The focus of the work of CPAG is UK policy and practice. There are other campaign and support organisations seeking to tackle poverty at an international level, such as Oxfam.

As Oxfam recognises, poverty is global problem. And in this broader context the levels of poverty and social exclusion experienced in the UK are nowhere near as serious as those found in many other parts of the world, where billions of people are seeking to survive on less than a dollar a day. Tackling global poverty is a much greater challenge than anti-poverty action in the UK or other Western countries, and the political will and economic resources required to tackle this global problem do not really exist, which is why the problem is so serious. In principle, however, global poverty is no different to national poverty. It is the product of structural forces which have led to a highly inequitable distribution of resources, meaning that, for the most part, those at the bottom of the social order are unable to make the same choices and participate in the same social activities as others who are better off.

Some people may be able to improve their lot and escape their poverty of course, and indeed the research evidence reveals that large numbers of people do move in and out of poverty over time. This also means, though, that more people are likely to be affected by poverty than are poor at any particular time, and that many more of us are at risk of poverty than we might realise. Poverty is therefore a problem of collective self-interest as well as moral concern, which is why the social insurance schemes developed in the early twentieth century were relatively popular as means of providing social security to protect citizens from poverty. In the UK in the twenty-first century, however, this National Insurance protection is less extensive and for many is not effective in preventing them from having to rely on minimal means-tested support. How to promote a renewed obligation to such collective self-protection is one of the key challenges facing any future commitment to collective welfare and social inclusion.

Health and illness

Health was identified by Doyal and Gough (1991) as one of two absolute human needs, as discussed in Chapter 2. In order to be effective human beings, we all need to be healthy – or at least as healthy as we can be. And most people would probably agree that promoting and protecting health should be one of the core goals of policies for welfare. This is a more complex issue in practice, however, because it depends upon what we mean by health, and what we think can, or should, be done to secure it – both the definition and the response are contested.

For a start, it is important to recognise that health is a relative phenomenon – even if in principle it is an absolute need. For instance, should we all aspire to the standards of health and fitness achieved by professional athletes, or is the sedentary and overweight office worker healthy if they are not suffering from any specific symptoms of illness? What we mean by illness can vary too, from a common cold to terminal cancer, with one obviously much more serious than the other. A distinction is also sometimes made between illness, disease and disability, although these too can overlap. See Box 3.4.

Box 3.4 Illness, disease and disability

Illness is a non-specific condition. For instance, I may have a cold and feel unwell, but this does not usually result in a medical diagnosis or treatment.

Disease is an identified medical condition, usually diagnosed by a doctor and leading to a medical intervention to cure or relieve it.

Disability is an ongoing condition which reduces our capacity to some extent. It may be caused by an illness or an accident, or it may be congenital. Disability, too, can often be alleviated or controlled by medical intervention.

What we mean by health, therefore, is complicated, and this extends to discussion of what the policy responses to it should be. The most important policy question is whether we should focus on treating illness or promoting health. The two are not mutually exclusive, of course – indeed, promoting health can help to reduce the experience, and the prevalence, of illness – but they do imply very different policy interventions. Health policy in the UK and elsewhere has tended to focus primarily upon the direct treatment of illness, rather than more indirect measures to promote health. This is understandable, because someone with a disease has a pressing need for treatment, and this is likely to manifest itself in a demand for health services to respond: if we have a high temperature we want a doctor to diagnose our disease, and if we break our leg we need a hospital service to reset it properly.

The bulk of health service activity and spending, therefore, is focused on general practitioner and hospital services to treat illness, disease and disability. Indeed, the National Health Service in the UK has sometimes disparagingly been referred to as a 'national illness service'. Nevertheless, the promotion of good health, and what is sometimes referred to as 'public health' policy, have always been a significant feature of health service provision. In recent decades they have received higher political and policy prominence, and targeted funding, even though in overall financial terms they are still the 'poor cousins' of health policy practice. Longer-term care for people with disabilities is also often seen as a lower policy priority, with funding generally provided by local authorities rather than the NHS. Funding for social care has always been much less than that for acute healthcare, although the lives of people with disabilities (or long-term diseases) can be much improved through the provision of support in their homes or, in more serious cases, in residential institutions.

What the complications over the priorities of health policy reveal, is that, as with welfare more generally, health is both an individual (or private) and a collective (or public) issue. As individuals we need to be healthy, as Doyal and Gough (1991) have argued, and we need policy interventions to help us to achieve this – particularly, of course, treatment when we are ill. However, we all have a collective interest in the maintenance of a healthy population, for instance, to reduce days lost to sickness at work and to ensure that all are capable of contributing appropriately to the common good. More specifically, promoting health and preventing disease are public problems. For instance, the prevention of smoking in public buildings protects non-smokers from the health risks associated with tobacco smoke (as well as discouraging smokers), and the use of public vaccination programmes prevents the spread of contagious diseases. Indeed the public benefits of vaccination were graphically revealed recently when the publication of bogus research linking the MMR (measles, mumps and rubella) vaccine to risks of autism in children led to a decline in take-up of the (free) vaccination by some parents, and consequently to a significant increase in cases of measles (potentially a fatal disease) in the child population (see Flaherty, 2011).

Collective action to prevent the spread of disease and to improve the environment for public health were among the first measures of health policy in the UK – for instance, the Public Health Act of 1848, which sought to tackle the poor sanitation and living conditions known to be linked to the spread of illness and disease. By contrast, individual health services in the nineteenth century were largely provided on a private or voluntary basis, mainly in the early hospitals built with private investment or charitable donations. It was only in the twentieth century that state welfare provision for health services was introduced on a widespread basis in the UK, culminating in the creation of the National Health Service (NHS) by the post-war Labour government in 1948.

The principle behind the NHS was the provision of comprehensive health services for all, free at the point of use and funded out of general taxation to which all would therefore contribute. It was the 'brainchild' of the Labour Cabinet Minister of the time, Aneurin (Nye) Bevan, who persuaded, sometimes reluctant, politicians and health professionals to support it. It has largely remained the most popular aspect of welfare provision in the country, as discussed in Chapter 7. In the 2015 election it was one of the few issues on which all political parties agreed public spending should be maintained or even increased.

Similar public health service provision can be found in most other advanced industrial nations, particularly in Europe, and the NHS has often been seen as a model of public healthcare for nations wanting to develop state provision for health needs. However, in the US public provision of healthcare has never really been developed. Most health providers in the US are private companies, and individuals can access these only through private health insurance; with only around 60 per cent of the population having such insurance cover, many are excluded from protection. As a result, there are only limited public schemes that provide healthcare: Medicare (for the over 65s) and Medicaid (for those who are poor); although the Obama administration has more recently sought to introduce a more comprehensive public insurance scheme for those not covered by private provision or targeted public support.

When the NHS was first introduced in the UK in 1948, there were concerns that people might not realise that they could access healthcare freely and advertising campaigns were used to encourage anyone who was ill to access NHS services. There was also an expectation that the wider availability of healthcare would over time reduce the need for services as the population became healthier. This did not happen, however; in fact demand for health services has grown gradually, and inexorably, since. In part, this is a product of the success of the service: more advanced forms of treatment have become available, and as a result people are living longer and have come to expect access to the latest technologies available. These demands have also put pressures on the funding base for the NHS, particularly because new machinery and new drugs are often expensive and in short supply.

The success of the NHS thus means that it can never meet all the demands placed on it by individual users and policy makers. As a result, health services have in effect had to be *rationed*, with doctors and other healthcare professionals determining what treatments and other services are available to their patients. In the UK this is now done directly through the budgets that doctors hold as members of clinical commissioning groups (CCGs), which are used to purchase services from other healthcare providers. To some extent, this rationing by doctors is of course inevitable, as they have much specialist knowledge of medical conditions and medical treatments, and patients will rely upon their advice and guidance in accessing healthcare – this is also to some extent true of all health professionals, including nurses and chemists. However, this knowledge can give doctors a paternalistic control over their patients, because both they and we tend to assume that they know what is best for us.

This paternalistic, or top down, control over healthcare by health professionals has been criticised for contributing to the 'provider culture' that is discussed in Chapter 4. It has led to the use of new public management (NPM) techniques to set targets for performance and spending, rather than relying on the judgement of professionals. It has also led to the introduction of some elements of market competition between providers to drive them to focus more directly on user needs, although for the most part these are really *quasi-markets* (see Le Grand and Bartlett, 1993), with the *provider* agencies, such as hospitals, competing for the resources controlled by the *purchaser* agencies, such as the CCGs, who hold the budgets for the treatments provided to patients.

Quasi-markets are also intended to provide a greater role for patient or user choice in healthcare, so that purchaser budgets can reflect the preferences of users for different services and service providers. This is rather limited in much healthcare, as in practice users are unlikely to have the knowledge and skills to determine what is best for their health needs. It has, however, become more widespread and more popular in social care, in the support provided (mainly at home) for people with disabilities or long-term diseases needing day-to-day support. Here there have even been moves to *personalise* services by giving a fixed level of resources (a personal budget) to the users themselves, which they can use to purchase services from public service providers – or even, perhaps, private or voluntary providers.

The use of private and voluntary providers within the health service has always had a more significant role than the model of a free and comprehensive public service might suggest. Private healthcare is available for those who can afford it and private insurance can be taken out to cover the fees charged for private treatments, with around 10 per cent of the UK population having some insurance cover, often provided through their employment. However, most of the cover provided is limited in scope, and in practice is supported indirectly by the NHS, which has trained the doctors and nurses that work in most private hospitals. Private healthcare is not therefore an alternative to the NHS, even for those who can afford it, and, as the US health insurance market reveals, market-based healthcare provision leads to discrimination and exclusion of some, usually those with greater needs and fewer resources.

The role of private companies in delivering health and social care has expanded in a different way in the last two decades or so, as some of the public services of the NHS and social care have been 'contracted out' to external providers, commissioned by state health and social care agencies to deliver these specified services for fixed periods of time. These contracts have also sometimes been offered to third sector or voluntary organisations, and have been part of broader attempts to open up public welfare to alternative providers, as discussed in Chapter 4.

The involvement of these alternative providers has sometime been criticised as a form of 'privatisation' of state services, which has the potential to undermine significantly the principle of the NHS as a free and comprehensive public service. Private providers may be able to make a profit out of delivering some of these services, although arguably that is not what motivates third sector providers, and these alternative providers are still delivering healthcare services free at the point of use and funded out of general taxation. In principle, they are therefore still part of public welfare services. Supporters of external commissioning argue that this further element of competition could make the service more efficient and provide greater choice for service users.

These recent changes to introduce quasi-markets and alternative providers need to be seen in the context of the continuing pressures of the rising demand for and cost of healthcare, as well as the continuing need to ration access to services and to find new ways to do this, while also seeking to promote innovation and efficiency. Public spending on healthcare in the UK has risen gradually since the introduction of the NHS, both in cash terms and as a proportion of GDP. This growth had slowed in the 1980s and 1990s, but expenditure was increased significantly in the 2000s by the Labour governments, taking spending up to around 9 per cent of GDP, which is about the average for health spending in OECD nations. Since 2010 public sector austerity measures have been putting pressure on this, and despite government claims to protect the NHS spending, it has in effect been frozen in cash terms, leading to cuts in budgets and a continuing expectation of what are called 'efficiency savings'.

No healthcare system can meet all the demands flowing from improving treatments and increased user expectations, a challenge that this book will return to discuss in more general terms in

Chapter 7. The recent attempts to open up provision to internal and external competition may help to promote innovation and change in some services. By challenging the 'provider culture' they may also give service users, and citizens more generally, some greater involvement in the production (or co-production) of services, an issue to which I will return in Chapter 4. Despite the cries of privatisation, these alternative providers remain within the collective provision of the NHS and related social care.

The NHS remains perhaps the most iconic example of popular and successful public welfare provision in the UK – and this is true of public health in many other countries too. Public support for collective investment in healthcare remains strong, and it is important to recognise and build on this to promote public welfare. The focus of this support is mainly on the services developed to respond to illness, disease and disability, rather than wider measures that might promote improved health such as safer working environments and improved diets. The measures taken to ban smoking in public places, to protect non-smokers and to discourage smokers, have been a successful example of the role that these wider measures can play in preventing disease and promoting healthy living. Such preventative measures need to play a more important role in future collective policy planning if the NHS is to move from being an (increasingly expensive) national illness service to part of a more general commitment to support public health.

Education and learning

After health, education is often the most popular feature of public welfare, as the attitude surveys discussed in Chapter 7 reveal. This is because we have all had experience of education and have benefited from it, and also probably because we recognise that we need to acquire important knowledge and skills to develop as human beings and to participate effectively in social relations. For instance, we need to be able to read and write to communicate indirectly with others, and in the twenty-first century we need to be able to understand and use information and communication technologies as well.

Like other aspects of welfare, education is both an individual and collective need. As individuals we need to acquire basic skills and knowledge, for instance, in English, mathematics and science. As individuals we also benefit directly and indirectly from this learning, for example, when we acquire qualifications, which are evidence of our knowledge and achievement and can be critically important in securing employment or getting access to further educational opportunities.

Education is also a collective need, however. An educated society is likely to be a more successful and productive one. We have a shared interest in all members of society reaching at least minimal standards of education, so that all can read public information and communicate with others, for example. More specifically, we have a collective interest in certain members of society achieving higher levels of knowledge and skills: we need, and value, well-trained doctors, teachers, engineers and others.

Investment in education to provide both general and specific knowledge and skills is thus part of our wider promotion of individual and collective welfare. This is sometimes referred to as investment in *human capital*, and we all have an interest in growing the extent and depth of human capital in our society. The commitment to public investment in education has therefore come to occupy a central place in the politics of welfare. This was graphically revealed in a speech made to the Labour Party Conference in 1996 by Tony Blair, who in the following year would become Prime Minister in the new UK Labour government. He said, "Ask me my three main priorities for government and I tell you: education, education and education."

Schools

Not surprisingly, therefore, education has been the focus of social policy intervention for some time. Although local schools existed before then, often run by churches, the Elementary Education Act of 1870 introduced public funding for establishing and running schools for all children aged five to 10, and in 1880 this elementary education was made compulsory. In 1902, as part of the early twentieth-century welfare reforms, responsibility for state education was passed to Local Education Authorities (LEAs), and in 1918 the age of compulsory education was raised to 14. Education was also at the centre of the welfare state reforms of the post-war years. The Education Act 1944 was the first of these changes, introduced by the wartime coalition government, but with strong Labour Party support. It extended secondary school education to all children up to the age of 15, to be provided by all LEAs in separate secondary schools; compulsory participation in secondary education was later extended to 16, then in the new century to 17 and later 18.

Since the 1980s, however, some aspects of marketisation have been introduced into state education – or rather quasi-markets, as in healthcare. This was achieved by permitting parents to choose which school to send their children to, rather than being allocated a place at the local school by the LEA, as had been the case in the past. In practice, this also meant that schools could now choose which pupils to admit, particularly if they were popular with parents and had a lot of pupils seeking a place. This introduced competition between schools (and between parents and children!). This was further fuelled by the publication of the examination results achieved by children at schools and the reports on them by the national inspection body, the Office for Standards in Education (Ofsted), from which 'league tables' could be constructed informing parents which were (supposedly) the best schools.

This marketisation has been taken further in the new century, by the power given to schools to leave LEA control altogether and become independent 'academies', and since 2010 by the establishment of entirely new 'free schools', which can be set up by any group of parents and supporters, but are guaranteed state funding on the same bases as established schools. As in healthcare, academies and free schools have extended the role of quasi-markets in public education. Their supporters have argued that this competition between schools will work to drive up standards, with all schools wanting to do better in order to ensure that they can still attract pupils. However, in the short-run at least, for those schools at the bottom of the league tables – and more importantly, perhaps, for those pupils within them – there may be a price to pay for this competition, as the funding linked to pupils is lost and schools become less and less able to attract both teachers and pupils. Some state schools are therefore undoubtedly 'better' than others.

Despite their independence from LEAs, academies and free schools all remain part of the state education system. However, genuinely private provision of education still exists within the UK. Private schools (sometimes misleadingly called 'public schools') offering separate provision in dedicated schools in return for fees paid by the parents of pupils have existed for a long time, in some cases preceding state education – for instance, the high profile schools at Eton and Harrow. Only around 7–8 per cent of the school age population attend such private schools, and these are generally those from the wealthiest and most privileged families, who can afford the high fees. As with healthcare, therefore, there is a limited private market for education, which is accessed mainly by the top 10 per cent or less of the population. And, as in healthcare, this private provision is supported indirectly by the public investment in the training of teachers, although 'public schools' are also subsidised by their exemption from some of the taxes that they would otherwise pay, because they are able to claim charitable status.

In the case of education in particular, this can have the effect of undermining the wider collective experience of, and commitment to, public provision. For many of the pupils educated in 'public schools', their relative exclusion from the collective experiences of their less privileged peers can give them a rather limited perspective on the social relations within which most people live, as well as providing them disproportionate success in securing places at the top universities and occupying some of the more influential positions in society – David Cameron, the Conservative Prime

Minister, went to Eton, and most of his Cabinet ministers also attended private schools.

Despite the existence of private education in 'public schools', the education that most people experience in state schools is, like healthcare, free at the point of use and collectively funded through taxation. The balance between private and public funding for public education is more complex in another area of learning, however: the higher education provided in universities.

Universities

University education has been around since the early days of the Oxford and Cambridge colleges in the fourteenth and fifteenth centuries. Nevertheless, at the beginning of the twentieth century there were just a handful of universities in the UK providing higher education to less than one per cent of the population. At the beginning of the century new universities were opened in most large cities, but even by the middle of the century in 1950 less than four per cent of the population had attended them. In the latter half of the century, however, particularly from the 1960s onwards, the number of universities in the country increased dramatically and attendance mushroomed – rising by the 2010s to almost 50 per cent of young people from the ages of 18 to 25.

The expansion of university education in the 1960s and 1970s was supported by public funding to cover the tuition provided (universities were publicly funded by government grants) and to provide for the living costs of students (through individual student grants). By the end of the century, however, the rapidly growing numbers of students was making this public support more and more expensive. Subsequently, over a series of years the student grants for living were replaced by loans, provided by government and repaid after graduation; students were also required to pay fees to cover (some of) the costs of tuition. In the 2010s these fees were raised to £9,000 a year, with students also getting a loan to cover the cost of these, which was to be repaid only when their income passed a threshold based on average wages. As a result of these changes, university students are now paying for most of the costs of their education, and are leaving universities with significant debts, which are likely to take them years, or decades, to pay off – although in the devolved administrations in Scotland, Wales and Northern Ireland lower fee levels are charged to students from within those countries.

Despite the growth in university attendance, however, only a proportion of the population experience higher education. The evidence suggests that by and large they can reap a significant reward from this in terms of better than average employment prospects and higher pay. However, the principle of charging a fee for public education is potentially a controversial one – there have been demonstrations opposing fees held by the National Union of Students. When they were introduced there was also concern in some quarters that fees for students might discourage some from going to university, although in practice the number of applications has remained high and this seems to be an unfounded fear. Hence, to a lesser extent, student fees complicate the argument about the individual and collective benefits of education. Of course doctors and (hence to a lesser extent) teachers will earn high salaries as a result of their qualifications, but we all rely on the availability of doctors, teachers and others who have acquired specialist knowledge and skills through university education. There is a collective benefit here, as well as the individual gain; arguably it is reasonable that we should all contribute to the costs of providing for this.

Nevertheless, with over 90 per cent of children in state schools, and almost 50 per cent of young people now going to university, the state education system remains a central part of public welfare in the UK. And we all continue to reap the individual and collective benefits of this investment in the expansion of human capital. However, as the move towards private fees and market competition reveal, the balance between public benefits and individual interests has been changing significantly over recent decades. The delivery of state education has become a more complex affair in twenty-first-century Britain – and a more differentiated and unequal one. However, it remains essential to ensuring that all can have access to learning to improve their, and our, human capital.

Summary

The provision of services to meet our key welfare needs is at the heart of public welfare and it constitutes the core of social policy. This chapter has outlined how poverty and social exclusion, health and illness, and education and learning have been identified and understood as both individual needs and social problems, and how public services have been developed to respond to these. These public services have also to some extent operated alongside private protection and voluntary action. They have also been affected by policy initiatives to introduce competition and alternative providers into state welfare, particularly in recent decades. This reveals that planning for social security, health and education have all involved a complex balance between collective investment and individual choice and responsibility – between the structures that we need to maintain the common good and the agency that all citizens have to shape their experience of the services they use. Nevertheless, these core services remain at the centre of our investment in public service provision and the promotion of welfare for all citizens.

Key texts

For a more detailed discussion of the main welfare issues, there are a number of social policy textbooks providing fairly comprehensive coverage of these and other social policy debates. These include Alcock with May (2014), Alcock et al (2016) and Baldock et al (2011). Spicker (2007) discusses the 'idea of poverty', and Unwin (2013) provides a passionate plea for why we should be concerned to 'fight' it. Ball's (2008) second edition of his exploration of 'the education debate' is a good introduction to the key policy issues here, and in the same series, Hunter (2008) is a similar introduction to health policy debates.

[handwritten: State V market.]

4

How should we deliver welfare?

In this chapter I examine some of the main practical issues to be overcome in delivering welfare. However great our commitment to meeting welfare needs, we need to ensure that the services that we develop to meet these can be delivered effectively and are accessible to those who use them. While Chapter 2 was concerned mainly with *what* should be the goals of welfare policy, this chapter is mainly concerned with *how* those policies operate. As I will explain, this has become a more significant feature of policy making and policy practice in recent decades, as providers, managers and governments have recognised that what matters most in practice is whether citizens can access the services that are intended to benefit them.

Distribution and redistribution

[handwritten: Robin Hood function.]

At the centre of our concerns about the welfare of citizens are the distribution and redistribution of resources. We need resources to meet our welfare needs. Yet, as I explained in Chapter 2 in discussing equality and inequality, resources are often unevenly distributed in society, with some people without sufficient means to meet all of their needs – and some with much more than they really need. And, as I argued, this could, and should, be addressed by seeking to reduce these massive disparities in income and wealth at source, through controls on income differentials and wealth holdings. However, we can also intervene to *re*distribute resources within society, to move them from those who have more than they need to those who do not have enough. It is such redistribution that has in fact been at the heart of most welfare policy.

Redistribution can involve the direct transfer of cash (or financial resources) collected from some in taxes and paid to others as benefits or credits; such cash transfers have been at the centre of welfare policy at least since the early days of the Poor Laws. However, redistribution can also take place through the provision of goods and services to those who cannot afford to pay for them, either free or at a subsidised rate – sometimes referred to as the 'social wage'. Redistribution is about moving resources from some people to others. It can take different forms and be based on different principles. In particular, there is a distinction between what academics call *vertical* and *horizontal* redistribution. See Box 4.1.

Box 4.1 Vertical redistribution and horizontal redistribution

Vertical redistribution is the transfer of resources from those who currently have more than they need to those who do not have enough – in simple terms from rich to poor. John Hills (2015) has referred to this as the 'Robin Hood principle', with some people contributing (perhaps unwillingly) so that others may benefit. Vertical redistribution can meet immediate need and help to reduce inequality, but it also implies a division between those who pay and those who receive – what Hills called the problem of 'them and us'. Vertical redistribution may be unpopular with the rich, who pay, and may stigmatise the poor, who benefit only because they cannot provide for themselves.

Horizontal redistribution is the transfer of resources across the life cycle, from people at some points in their lives, when they have spare resources, to other times, when they do not. Hills has called this the 'savings bank approach'. In practice, however, horizontal redistribution does not save people's money like a bank or an insurance scheme. Rather, it transfers resources across different age groups within the population, collecting money from those in work with incomes and providing for those at risk of being in need because they cannot work or secure a sufficient income. Child Benefit and retirement pensions are the main examples of horizontal redistribution within the social security system, and they constitute by far the largest proportion of spending (or redistribution)

in the UK. Arguably, the provision of public services like health and
education is also a form of horizontal redistribution, particularly because
they are not restricted to those who cannot afford to pay, and because
all of us will be likely to benefit from them at some point in our lives.

Vertical and horizontal redistribution are quite different in terms
of both their underlying principles and their practical effects.
Nevertheless, both are widely employed in social policy in the UK
and in all other welfare regimes – although the balance between
the two varies in different countries. Indeed, it is the balance
between vertical and horizontal redistribution which is one of
the key distinguishing features between welfare regimes. Vertical
redistribution is more common in *liberal* regimes like the USA,
where levels of inequality are higher, and horizontal redistribution
more common in *social democratic* and *corporatist* regimes like Sweden
and Germany, where inequality is lower and public services are
more likely to be available to all. For further discussion and analysis
of the differences between these international welfare regimes, see
Esping-Andersen (1990).

Vertical redistribution requires us to take decisions about levels of
equality and inequality, about who should contribute, how much
they should contribute, and who should benefit. This is a matter
of principle: who should pay for whom? It also has significant
practical implications. Deciding who should pay, and how much,
goes to the heart of policies on the forms and levels of taxation.
To what extent should we ensure that taxation is 'progressive', so
that those with the most resources pay the highest level?

In the UK the largest form of taxation, income tax, is progressive
to an extent, with those at the bottom of the income distribution
paying none, the majority in the middle paying 20 per cent, those
on higher incomes paying 40 per cent, and those on the highest
incomes paying 45 per cent. This is a pattern that has changed
over time. The highest tax rate was 50 per cent under the previous
Labour government, reduced to 45 per cent under the Coalition;
and prior to the tax reforms of the 1980s the top rate had been

much higher, at over 90 per cent for the very highest earnings. Income tax is therefore not as progressive as it used to be in the UK, and not as progressive as it is in some social democratic welfare regimes in places like Scandinavia. What is more, income tax is only one source of contributions to public spending. National Insurance contributions also act as a tax on incomes, and these are not progressive across income levels. Taxes on spending, such as Value Added Tax (VAT), apply equally to all who purchase the goods covered by the tax.

In practice, therefore, deciding who should contribute and how much they should pay is a complex and politically charged issue – in effect, it is not just the 'rich' who pay for the 'poor'. However, vertical redistribution also requires us to decide who is to benefit from transfers of resources. If these are to go only to those in need, then some means of assessing their need, and their inability to provide for this themselves, will have to be applied. For the most part this is done through a *means-test*. This is a formal audit of someone's resources in order to determine how much income (and any savings) they have and therefore how much additional support should be transferred to them. This usually involves filling in a form to declare income and resources, and entitlement to support depends on how far these fall below levels fixed within the different welfare schemes.

Means-tests are used primarily to determine entitlement to social security benefits, such as Jobseeker's Allowance, Income Support or Housing Benefit, but they are also used to assess entitlement to a range of other benefits and services that are targeted at people on low incomes. Means-tests (and vertical redistribution more generally) can lead to the 'them and us' culture described by Hills (2015). That is, a separation between the interests of those who are paying for welfare, and those who are receiving it. As mentioned in Box 4.1, this can make vertical redistribution less popular within welfare policy, because of a belief that only a few at the bottom are benefiting from it.

[handwritten: Horizontal redistribution]

In practice, however, people move in and out of poverty and low income. It is not always the same people who are at the bottom and are the beneficiaries of vertical redistribution. Indeed, as Hills (2015, p 266) points out, around a half of the UK population are likely to receive a means-tested benefit at some point in their lives. Therefore, the notion of 'them and us' welfare, driven by vertical redistribution, is a myth, and, as mentioned above, UK social policy is based on both vertical and horizontal distribution of resources (as are other welfare regimes).

In fact, overall, horizontal redistribution is more important than vertical redistribution in meeting our wide range of welfare needs, as Hills' (2015) analysis reveals. Transferring resources between people at different points in their life cycle and at times of different needs means that in this respect we are 'all in this together'; and this becomes clearer when we take a longer-term perspective and look across the life course. As children, and perhaps as parents, we have all benefited from the support provided by Child Benefit (although, as explained below, this is now no longer true for all), and we also all hope to benefit from pension support in our older age. All citizens benefit from education, at least as children, and for some later in life too, and, although less predictable, we are also likely to need provision for health and perhaps social care needs.

When we take an even longer-term view, across generations and social cohorts, then the potential role of horizontal redistribution becomes even more important. There is some scope for social mobility within society – some people do make the journey 'from rags to riches', and indeed the other way round. Overall, however, social mobility is rather limited in British society, with most of those born into families with low incomes likely to experience this themselves as adults, and most of the children of the better-off likely to end up at the top too (Hills, 2015, Ch 7). And when we look across generational cohorts, other potential inequities emerge. Much has been made recently of the so-called 'baby boomer' generation, those born in the years shortly after the Second World War, who over the course of their lifetime have benefited from the public services of the new welfare state, relatively high and stable employment and potentially generous occupational pensions in retirement. This cohort is contrasted with 'generation X', born in the 1960s and 1970s, and 'generation Y', born in the 1980s and 1990s, both of which have experienced different political and economic contexts, with higher levels of redundancy and unemployment, reductions in public services, and declining values of private pensions.

These are to some degree generalisations of course. Not all of the baby boomer generation experienced stable employment and have generous pensions, and some in generations X and Y may have both of these. However, these differences in the circumstances and experiences of different generational cohorts reveal the longer-term implications of the need for horizontal redistribution. In practice it is generations X and Y who will be paying the pensions of the baby boomers, and providing all the goods and services that they spend these on – and as explained in Chapter 6, with the older generation constituting a larger and larger proportion of the population as life expectancy expands, this will be a growing redistributional burden. Longer-term planning needs to ensure that future generations can afford such redistribution, and in time will be able to benefit from it. This requires long-term commitments to a collective approach to the transfer of resources across the generations, as well as investment in the collective resources (the common goods such as houses, hospitals, schools and universities) that can support future generations.

This long-term approach to redistribution reveals the importance of a collective approach towards meeting welfare needs and the redistribution of resources that is needed to achieve this. We could not ever meet these long-term challenges as individuals, purchasing services when needed from the private market and taking out insurance for future support. The private markets for healthcare and education serve less than ten per cent of the potential demand for these, and rely upon public services to provide the training and experience for the professional staff that they employ. Although private pension provision has grown, and is now supported by government, it is still predicated upon the assumption that state pensions will be available as an income floor for all. And private insurance provision for unemployment and long-term sickness have never been developed in the UK, or in other advanced welfare regimes, because, as discussed in Chapter 8, they are not a commercially viable vehicle for providing protection for all those who might need it. We need redistribution through public benefits and public services.

Hills' extensive analysis of the need for the transfer of resources through public services and welfare support as the most efficient and effective way of meeting our welfare needs ends with a quote that reminds us of the overall collective nature of this redistribution:

> As a result of this variation of circumstances over our lives between good times and bad times, most of us get back something at least close to what we pay in over our lives towards the welfare state. When we pay in more than we get out, we are helping our parents, our children, ourselves at another time – and ourselves as we might have been, if life had not turned out quite so well for us. In that sense we are all – or nearly all – in it together. (Hills, 2015, p 286)

Universalism and selectivity

The redistribution of resources is therefore at the heart of the welfare policy, through the transfer of money and the provision of goods and services (the social wage). However, if resources are to be distributed, either directly or indirectly, we need to decide how to do this. Here there is a choice to be made between the *universal* provision of resources to all or the *selective* distribution of these only to those who need them – see Box 4.2.

Box 4.2 Universal and selective services

Universal services are provided equally to all who need, or expect, to benefit from them. State education in schools and most NHS services are universal, and so too was Child Benefit until it was withdrawn from higher rate taxpayers in 2013.

Selective services restrict access to those identified as having particular needs or being in particular circumstances. This is sometimes referred to as *targeting* support on those in need. It is widely used in social security to target benefits on those in need using means-tests, but it is also employed in a range of other service areas to restrict these to particular groups of users or to those on low incomes.

The principles behind these forms of distribution are different and they lead to different outcomes within welfare services. However, both are employed within the UK, and in most other welfare regimes. As with horizontal versus vertical redistribution, here too it is the balance between the two which is most important in determining the overall shape of welfare policy within regimes. For instance, although most services within the NHS are universal, when charges for prescriptions for drugs were introduced, exemptions from these charges (free prescriptions) were provided, targeted on particular groups such as children, the elderly and those on low incomes. Since the devolution of health policy in the UK, however, the separate administrations in Scotland, Wales and Northern Ireland have all abandoned this selectivity and provided free prescriptions for all – and in England the wide targets for exemptions mean that in practice around 88 per cent of prescriptions are provided free.

The advantage of selectivity, at least in principle, is that resources can be targeted on those most in need, which may be particularly important if resources are constrained– – although, as the free prescription policy reveals, if targets are too broad, they may not be very practical. Targeting can be based on people's circumstances or condition – such as age group for free prescriptions or physical condition for disability benefits like the Personal Independence Payment for people who need help with care or mobility – or targeting can be based on low income, using means-testing. In all cases, however, targets need to be identified and defined, and inevitably lines will have to be drawn between those who can benefit and those who cannot – with those outside the lines, however close, missing out.

This targeting leads to particular problems in the case of means-testing, as suggested when discussing vertical redistribution above. Means-tests are inevitably quite complex, to ensure that all sources of income and capital are taken into account, usually involving the completion of complex application forms. Potential applicants need to be able to identify their possible entitlement and go through the process of making a claim. Many fail to do this for a variety of reasons, leading to what is referred to as 'non-take-up'. This is a significant problem in principle, since it means that people who are likely to be poor and in need are not getting the resources supposedly targeted at them. It is also a problem in practice, with government estimates of non-take-up of the main means-tested social security benefits suggesting that around 15 per cent are not getting this support.

Means-tested benefits are targeted on those on low incomes, with the implication that these people are unable to provide fully for themselves because they are poor. Deacon and Bradshaw (1983) once referred to such support as being 'reserved for the poor', and they pointed out that as a result this often carried a significant stigma, associated with poverty, need and dependency. This can further fuel the 'them and us' ideology criticised by Hills (2015) and, of course, it is likely to add to the problems of non-take-up if people are fearful of being identified as poor and having to depend on targeted support. What is more, it contrasts with the much lower levels of fraud and abuse, which are less than one per cent of all benefit expenditure (Hills, 2015, p 263). Non-take-up of means-tested benefits is therefore a much more significant problem than fraudulent claiming – yet this is not the message found in much popular media discourse on the 'problems of scrounging'.

There is another more complex and contradictory problem with the operation of means-tested support, however, which flows from the fact that entitlement to support is dependent upon low income. Because of the means-tested support that claimants receive, particularly people who are unemployed, this may mean that this support turns out to be more than the low wages that they could expect in employment. And, where this support is paid to people who are on low wages, it may discourage them from improving their pay since this would reduce their entitlement to benefit. These problems are referred to as the *unemployment* and *poverty* traps – see Box 4.3.

Box 4.3 The unemployment and poverty traps

The unemployment trap is the situation faced by a person, or more usually a family, who are unemployed and receiving a range of means-tested benefits, linked to their circumstances, including perhaps Housing Benefit to cover some or all of their rent. This may add up to a larger weekly or monthly income that they would be likely to get in the type of low-paid employment that may be available to them. Therefore, they are 'trapped' in unemployment. This problem has been recognised for some time, and has been addressed by the provision of additional means-tested support to supplement the wages of those on low incomes, linked to the costs of children and housing rent, and now in the UK called tax credits. However, this creates another problem.

The poverty trap is the consequence of the (perverse) incentive effect of tax credits or other benefits to subsidise low wages. This support is based on wage levels, so that if these rise, support must be withdrawn. This reduces the value of any additional income, and when combined with other tax and National Insurance contributions can lead to 'marginal tax rates' (the amount of take-home income lost from any additional pay) of over 90 per cent – much higher than the 45 per cent tax rate levied on the highest paid. The poverty trap is therefore a disincentive for the low paid to improve their circumstances at work. Additionally, it is a disincentive for employers to increase wages, since they are benefiting indirectly from the public subsidy to the low wages they are paying. This means that those on low pay are effectively trapped on their low incomes, with increases in pay making little real difference to take-home income across a significant spectrum of the low wage work force.

These traps are structural features of means-tested selectivity. The targeting of resources onto defined sections of the population is always going to lead to these being withdrawn if the circumstances that have led to their entitlement change. It might be argued that this is not such a significant problem in principle, because arguably their changed circumstances have removed people's need for support. In practice, however, as the poverty trap demonstrates, it is not that simple – in particular, of course, because targeting is always going to leave some just outside the benefit net, even though their circumstances may be little better than those just below them within it.

Incentives are generally regarded as an important feature of economic policy, justifying high wages for some to encourage them to work harder. Yet at the bottom of the income distribution, selectivity produces incentives that have the perverse effect of discouraging people from seeking higher wages – and discouraging employers from paying them. By contrast, universal services go to all, so there are no problems of take-up or stigma, or perverse incentives to 'remain' within the target groups. Universal services are therefore also easier to deliver and to use. The major criticism of them is that they are expensive, at least in principle, as they provide resources and services to those who do not need them or who could afford to pay for them on the open market.

It is for this reason that in 2013 the UK coalition government restricted the previously universal Child Benefit to those with incomes below the 40 per cent higher rate tax band. This meant, however, that the tax returns of both parents had to be checked to determine whether the parent receiving the benefit (usually the mother) was entitled to it. This is more intrusive, and costly to administer, than paying the benefit to all families. It also means that those on higher incomes are no longer receiving any public support for their childcare costs; and there is a principle involved here about our collective interest in, and investment in, all children.

Children are part of the future for us all, and arguably all children should be supported in the same way. If the parents of some have high incomes, then these incomes could be taxed to pay for this, as for other benefits and services, and wealthy non-parents could be taxed too, for they also have an investment in our children and their futures. It is all children who will form the future generation who will pay the taxes and provide the services that we will all benefit from – and we will benefit from these whether or not we have children of our own. In this sense, universal support is linked to the horizontal redistribution of resources discussed above, and to what has sometimes been called 'generational justice'.

There is also an important practical, or political, dimension to universal provision. Because all receive it, all have a vested interest in maintaining it, and maintaining its value and accessibility. It is this universal interest in the NHS and state education that to a significant extent explains why these are generally rated as the most popular features of welfare provision, as discussed in Chapter 7. We have all been to school, and visited a GP, and probably been to hospital – and we have done so without having to count the costs or prove that we were entitled to benefit.

Universal provision is therefore at the heart of collective welfare: from all, for all. And it is cheaper to administer because there is no need to identify targets and prove entitlement, which is part of the rationale for decisions by the devolved administrations of Scotland, Wales and Northern Ireland to remove charges for NHS prescriptions. However, it has come under threat from the argument that, especially when the pressure on public resources is great, welfare services should be targeted on those in most need. The scope of such selectivity has expanded significantly in the last three or four decades in the UK, and in most other welfare regimes, in particular, within social security. Making the case for universal welfare, though simpler in theory, has therefore become more difficult in practice.

Producers and users

The principles of universalism and selectivity provide different, and potentially conflicting, bases for the distribution of welfare services. They are not the only factors influencing how services and support are provided and accessed, however. All services must be provided or delivered, and traditionally much of the academic and policy concern with the delivery of welfare has been on supporting and controlling the provision of services, and the agencies and individuals working to provide them.

Thus we invest in the infrastructure for the provision of services – schools, hospitals, jobcentres and benefit offices. And these days we invest too in the IT systems that operate within these, although in practice there have often been problems with the large-scale IT projects commissioned to support services like the NHS or social security benefits. As I explained in Chapter 1, these are examples of the common goods which underpin collective welfare support. We also invest in the people who work in these services. This involves professional training for doctors, nurses and teachers, and the specification and maintenance of professional standards. More generally, it also includes the regulation and management of all service providers, which, as I discuss below, has become ever more extensive in recent decades.

We all need, and probably want, good schools and hospital buildings and equipment, and we expect those working within these to be appropriately trained and supported. The focus of much social policy has therefore been on ensuring the availability and quality of this provider base. However, this focus has been criticised for leading to what became called a 'provider culture' within welfare services. Because doctors and teachers are trained professionals, they know what is best for us, and because they have been trained and paid to provide a service to us, this will ensure that we benefit from it.

However, this *provider* culture has been criticised for overlooking the interests and perspectives of the *users* of welfare. At the end of the day, it is whether the users get the services and support that they need, and are entitled to, which is critical to the effective provision of welfare, and the professionalism and organisation of services should be geared to the needs of users. But sometimes, it is argued, this is not the case. The grand staircase up to the town hall can exclude users with some disabilities, and the nine-to-five opening times may prevent some employed workers from getting to service providers; bureaucratic inertia may frustrate user enquiries ('your file has been sent to another department'); and the condescending manner of some professionals (the hospital consultant who does not know the names of their patients) may belittle those wanting to pursue their rights to be served.

In 1990 a group of academics identified problems like these as potential barriers to people 'consuming public services' (Deakin and Wright, 1990), and argued that there was a problem with welfare services that were being delivered *to* people, rather than provided *for* them. This has been followed by campaigning from some user groups – notably, for example, those with disabilities (see Campbell and Oliver, 1996) – to raise the profile of user interests in welfare, and to pose the question of 'whose welfare' should be at the centre of policy planning (Beresford et al, 2011).

Motivation and agency

Implicit, and often explicit, in this user criticism of the provider culture is the allegedly unhelpful, or even hostile, attitudes and practices of some welfare providers. This seems to some extent counterintuitive. Surely we would expect those working in public services to be motivated to meet the needs of service users – is that not why they chose these careers in the first place? And, indeed, they most probably are motivated to help. However, as in any organisational *structure*, the actions taken to deliver services are taken by *agents*, and the ideals and practices of agents will inevitably vary.

In an analysis of the role of motivation and agency in public services Le Grand (2003) characterised the different attitudes and actions of those working in provider organisations as a contrast between *knights* and *knaves*. Public services workers who were dedicated to responding to and meeting the needs of the users of their services were displaying altruistic, knightly, behaviour; this was assumed to be the case particularly in the early post-war years of the welfare state. By contrast, public service workers could be side-tracked into a more knavish approach, focused on belief in their own abilities and geared to protecting their established working practices, and in extreme circumstances their jobs. Some have argued that this is an almost inevitable consequence of the growth of the large bureaucracies needed to deliver comprehensive public services, where the allegiance of workers moves from the users to the provider agencies, who then acquire a vested interest in protecting, and indeed expanding, their bureaucratic 'empires' – referred to by economists as 'public choice theory'.

Le Grand argued that this was accentuated by the moves towards new public management (NPM) practices in public services (which I discuss in more detail below), as this meant that workers would be under pressure to meet management targets, rather than respond directly to user demands. He pointed out, though, that both knights and knaves could be found within most public service providers, and indeed that individuals might at different times display both knightly and knavish tendencies. He also argued that there was a tendency within public services to treat users like pawns (further mixing up the chess and playing card metaphor!), and that this was particularly likely to be the case in the target-driven culture of NPM.

This meant that the users were regarded as the passive recipients of welfare, and that their agency was being overlooked or ignored. Le Grand was critical of this and argued that public services should aim to offer more power and control to users, particularly by giving them more choice over the services providers delivering welfare services to them. He characterised this as transforming service users from *pawns* into *queens*. The American economist Hirschman (1970) had earlier provided a similar critique of the treatment of users within the provider culture of public services. Users were pawns, in Le Grand's terms, because according to Hirschman they did not have the right of exit or voice in the services that they accessed.

Exit meant the availability of alternative providers of services, and the right of users to leave (or exit from) current providers to choose another who would offer them a better, or more desirable, service. Implicit in this right of exit was the existence of the role of market discipline in pressuring providers to improve the services they were offering, and it has led to significant moves towards *marketisation* within public services to seek to offer more choice to users, as I will return to discuss below.

Giving users a *voice* in shaping the services provided for them is an alternative means of empowering them to the introduction of market-based competition. It may be particularly important in transforming users from pawns to queens where markets are not operating, and especially where alternative providers cannot be developed, as is the case in many areas of social policy, such as social security or acute healthcare. Empowering users though exit and voice are not mutually exclusive responses to the provider culture, however; both have been increasingly widely pursued within the UK, and elsewhere, in recent decades to challenge and change many of the established provider practices of delivering welfare.

Regulation, targets and inspection

The most pervasive and influential responses to the public service challenges identified by critics like Le Grand and Hirschman have been the moves since the 1980s to introduce more extensive controls over providers through what came to be called new public management (NPM; see Pollitt, 1990; Flynn, 2012). NPM drew on the lessons that could supposedly be learnt from the management techniques and practices that had been developed in private businesses operating in the open market, where it was assumed that market discipline would have led to improvements in organisational structures and cultures. The major shift that this brought to public service provision was a move from the *administration* of services to the *management* of providers – see Box 4.4.

Box 4.4 Administration and management

Administration is concerned to ensure that services are established and that the professionals providing them are adequately supported in their work. Power over services lies primarily with professionals and administrators support them.

Management is concerned to ensure that services are delivered efficiently and effectively, and that professionals are aware of the objectives that they should be seeking to achieve and are accountable for their delivery of these. Power over services lies primarily with managers, who direct the work of professionals.

This change predominantly took the form of greater regulation of service provision through the setting of targets and the auditing of performance. Rather than professionals deciding service priorities and outcomes, these were set by managers as performance targets, which were be specified in 'indicators' of achievement, sometimes with 'milestones' set to measure progress towards final achievement. These could include things like the waiting times for hospital visits or the numbers of people recruited onto training courses for the unemployed.

What seems like a good idea in theory, to set specified targets for service delivery, does not always work out so well in practice, however:

- *First*, there is the question of who is to set the targets – in practice usually managers, not professionals, let alone users.

- *Second*, there is the problem of the nature of the targets set – too soft and providers can meet them easily, too hard and non-achievement will look like failure.
- *Third*, and most important perhaps, once targets for performance have been set, then activity can become geared to meeting the indicators and milestones, rather than to the broader needs and demands of service users.

At the end of the day, what matters most is the success of hospital treatment, not the time spent waiting for it; the number of people getting jobs, not the number of those completing the training course. At the beginning of the century Boyle (2001) published a trenchant critique of the impact of such target setting, which he called *The tyranny of numbers*, where he argued that numerical targets could never capture users' needs and would inevitably distort the delivery of public services.

The other significant change that flowed from NPM was the development of auditing of public services in order to provide an independent check on service activities and outcomes, and to hold providers to account in a way that the individual users of services would not be able to. It was also based on ensuring that providers were accountable too to those who were paying for the services they were delivering, in particular, of course, to government agencies and to the taxpayers that they indirectly represented. This accountability through audit goes beyond the narrow numerical targets of performance management, although it can include use of numerical measures of performance. Rather, it is based on reporting to independent auditors, perhaps together with inspection by them of provider organisations and activities.

In the UK the National Audit Office (NAO) provides independent scrutiny of the activities of central government departments, and the Audit Commission used to exercise a similar function for local government and other non-departmental government bodies. However, the Audit Commission was abolished in 2015 by the Coalition government, who argued that the scrutiny it provided was not securing value for money. This was clearly something of a backlash against the intrusive (and it was argued expensive) impact of this NPM control over public services from a government that was also critical of some of the target setting in public services and more inclined to see market competition as the most effective means of improving service standards.

The Coalition did, however, retain many of the more service-focused inspection regimes, which had been the most influential means of independent review of public services. The most well known is the Office for Standards in Education (Ofsted) which since 1992 has been making regular assessments of the performance of schools. This has included regular visits to observe the teaching and management of schools, plus assessment of attainment against a range of performance indicators, including pupils' exam performance. Schools are then rated on a scale from 'outstanding' to 'requires improvement', and the results are published on the Ofsted website.

Ofsted reports and performance indicators can then be used to rank schools and create league tables. In this way, regulation and inspection has also encouraged competition and marketization in school education. The same is true in other services such as universities (by the Higher Education Funding Council) and NHS trusts (by the Care Quality Commission), and these league tables can be employed by users to act more like queens than pawns in choosing the service providers who they think will deliver the best service.

However, as critics such as Clarke and Newman (Clarke et al, 2007) have pointed out, the impact of managerialism on public services has reduced the scope for knightly activity by professionals and undermined their specialist knowledge and service commitment. It has also tended to treat users as consumers or customers in a marketplace, rather than as active agents shaping and controlling service performance. What is more, in many services real market choice does not exist, and the knowledge and power that users need to act as discerning customers is not something that many can command. For instance, parents may want to choose the best performing school for their children, but league tables have made the highest ranked schools so popular that they have massive excess demand for places. This means that it is the schools that choose their pupils, rather than the other way round, and those with the resources to move their family to areas where 'good schools' can be found will be able to benefit most from this.

Sectors and providers

Marketisation of welfare services can in principle, however, provide a response to Hirschman's concern over the lack of 'exit' for consumers of monopoly public services. In theory, if there are alternative providers, then users can move to these if they are unhappy with the service they are getting from their current provider. Alternative providers give users *choice*, and through the exercise of choice they may also gain more *control* over the services they receive, as providers will need to adapt their services to meet demand if they wish to retain their customers. In Le Grand's terms, markets can make users more like queens, and Le Grand has been a supporter of the promotion of alternative providers in welfare services, notably in health, acting as an advisor to both the UK Labour and Coalition governments.

The quasi-markets introduced in health and education, discussed in Chapter 3, have provided an element of choice in what remain publicly provided services, although in reality this is limited, as it depends upon users having the knowledge and judgement to choose between alternative providers. In some areas this means that users still have to rely on professionals to act as 'proxy purchasers' for them, most notably in health in the role played by GPs in Clinical Commissioning Groups purchasing health services from NHS trusts. And, as mentioned above, in the case of schools where demand outstrips supply, choice can become illusory for many parents.

Alternative providers can also exist outside of the public sphere. For instance, there are private providers operating commercially, for profit, in the wider market, and there are voluntary, or non-profit, organisations operating in what is generally referred to as the third sector. Commercial and third sector provision of welfare services has a long history. It has always operated alongside public welfare, and in many fields preceded the development of state provision. For instance, private schools ('public schools') and voluntary schools (often run by churches) existed before state education was introduced, as discussed in Chapter 3. Voluntary organisations were also often the pioneers of other new forms of welfare provision, for example, the National Society for the Prevention of Cruelty to Children (NSPCC) and Barnardo's providing child protection in the nineteenth century, and hospices providing end of life care in the twentieth.

In the last two decades or so, however, there has been a significant growth in the role of commercial and third sector providers of welfare, following the contracting out of some public services and the commissioning of alternative providers to supplement, or replace, state welfare. Commissioning of alternative providers was encouraged in the UK by the Labour governments of the 2000s under their 'third way' approach, to increase user choice and control through the promotion of the mixed economy of welfare provision outlined in Chapter 1. It was expanded even more rapidly after 2010 under the Coalition, who published a White Paper in 2011 on 'opening up' public services, and contracted out provision in a number of major areas of welfare, such as employment support for the long-term unemployed and probation support for offenders and ex-offenders.

It is in health and especially social care, where the main extension of alternative provision has developed, driven by local commissioning from local authorities and clinical commissioning groups and trusts. And it is also here where third sector provision has been particularly important, including policy initiatives to encourage groups of public sector workers to (re)create themselves as independent (mutual) organisations, so that services can be transferred to them. A taskforce to promote such mutualisation was established by the Coalition government, led by Julian Le Grand.

Despite the opening up of public services by recent governments in the UK, however, much welfare provision remains in public hands. And despite the claims that commercial providers may be more efficient than public monopolies, or that third sector providers could be more innovative or responsive to user needs and preferences, there is little reliable evidence that the exit offered by alternative providers has given users much greater choice or control over welfare services.

Of course, ultimately, what matters is whether users can get access to the services that they need or want, not who has the right, or the responsibility, to provide them. But the relatively limited scope of private and third sector welfare reminds us of the important role that public provision continues to play in meeting our collective welfare needs – not the least because, as explained in Chapter 8, in a democracy only state agencies have a mandate to operate for and on behalf of all citizens. And no matter how extensive alternatives are, it is state support that must always be available to provide a safety net for citizens when other providers fail to materialise, or fail to deliver.

Personalisation and co-production

Given the limitations in alternative providers as a means of empowering the users of welfare services through 'exit', there have been more moves in recent times to increase the 'voice' of users in the design and delivery of services. One of the criticisms made by the user campaigns of the provider culture in public welfare was the argument that control over the resources to deliver most welfare services remained with the providers, on the assumption that they knew best what users needed. While this may be true to an extent – for instance, in the case of acute hospital treatment – it also meant that users generally had no say in how resources were deployed on their behalf. If, it was argued, these resources could be transferred to the users themselves, so that they had a notional 'personal budget' to purchase the services they wanted, then this could allow them to decide on the priorities that they most valued and to choose the providers that most closely meet their needs and preferences. In other words, it would permit them to *personalise* their access to collective welfare.

The use of individual budgets and other related mechanisms to personalise services has been developed in a number of services areas, most notably in social care, as discussed by Needham (2011; Needham and Glasby, 2014). It has the potential to transfer power and control to users, although only, of course, if they have the knowledge and ability to manage their budgets and make informed and effective choices between providers; and for many users, especially the vulnerable users of some social care services, this may not be the case. Additionally, if collective resources are dispersed in this way, then some of the 'economies of scale' of collective provision may be lost, because providers will not be able to plan and invest in services across a range of known beneficiaries, and will only be able to react to the vagaries of individual preferences.

Transferring the public resources of collective welfare to individual users may not, therefore, always be a very effective way of giving them a voice in the design and delivery of public services. This could be mitigated, however, if user involvement in, and control over, service provision was shared with providers. In simple terms, this is what the proponents of *co-production* wish to develop. Co-production is where the users and providers of services work together to deliver them; it could involve co-design, where they work together to shape and structure them too.

Co-production is not actually such a new phenomenon, although it is a relatively new term. Users and producers have always worked together in the delivery of welfare. Doctors can prescribe drugs to help cure us when we are ill, and we may get these drugs free depending on where we live or who we are, but we still have to take the drugs and (as it usually says on the packet) complete the course of treatment even when the symptoms appear to have abated. More generally of course, we can avoid illness and help to treat ourselves by keeping fit, avoiding risky activities (like smoking or over-eating), and identifying and responding to the symptoms of illness. In this way, we all co-produce our health.

However, the more recent proponents of co-production see the recognition of the role that users play in the take-up and delivery of the services from which they benefit as becoming a more structural feature of all service planning, together with the more formal involvement of users in decisions about the design and delivery of welfare services too, through individual and collective forums for engagement and consultation. This recognises that the production (or co-production) of public services involves a changing relationship between providers and users. The delivery of public services is about changing relations rather than delivering a product (Osborne et al, 2013), and in this sense the interests and activities of users are intrinsically at the heart of what is provided.

Co-production and personalisation thus have the potential to challenge the provider culture of public welfare services by giving users, and citizens more generally, a greater voice in these. In Le Grand's terms, this will help turn the pawns into queens. If this also involves giving users more choice between service providers then it could further provide a renewed basis for citizens and users to recognise and identify with the practical values of the collective provision of welfare for them as individuals. This is something to which I shall return in Chapter 8. Nevertheless, it must be set in the context of the continuing need to recognise that, however they are delivered, public welfare services must also be paid for.

Paying for welfare

The provision of welfare involves the distribution and redistribution of resources. Resources are needed to provide direct support, such as social security benefits, and to deliver services, such as health and education. As discussed above, this encompasses both horizontal and vertical redistribution. Redistribution is collective action to promote welfare. It requires resources to be collected to pay for the benefits and services provided, and the growth of state welfare in the twentieth century was based upon the collection of resources through the state to pay for this redistribution.

For the most part, public resources are collected through taxation, by governments and on behalf of citizens – or taxpayers, as commentators wishing to emphasise the collective source of resources sometimes call them. Taxation includes both *direct* taxes, on income, and *indirect* taxes, on spending. Income taxes are generally more progressive with the higher paid contributing a larger proportion of their income and the lowest paid exempted from income tax altogether, whereas indirect taxes, in particular Valued Added Tax (VAT), are more regressive as they apply to a wide range of goods which most people need to buy. Both direct and indirect taxation are used to collect resources, with income tax itself contributing only about a quarter, as the pie chart in Figure 4.1 reveals. What is more, the balance of these has changed over time, with indirect taxes becoming more important in the UK in recent times, particularly VAT, which was increased by the Coalition government despite their commitment to using spending cuts rather than tax rises to reduce the public sector deficit, as discussed in Chapter 7.

Taxation is a collective investment in welfare, as well as in other public goods such as transport infrastructure and defence. We might expect, therefore, that it would be popular as an investment in the common good. In practice, however, there has always been some resistance to the 'imposition' of taxation by governments, especially income tax, which is more transparent to those who pay it. This resistance has become more pronounced in the UK since the 1980s, linked to the growing influence of neoliberalism with its individualist, anti-government, sentiments. Governments have become more reluctant to increase taxation in order to fund expanding public expenditure, a phenomenon that can be found in many welfare capitalist regimes in the late twentieth and early

Figure 4.1: Public expenditure: receipts 2015/16

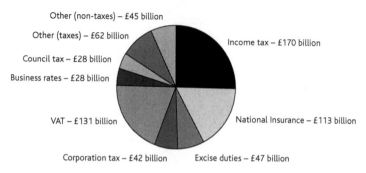

Other (non-taxes) – £45 billion

Other (taxes) – £62 billion

Council tax – £28 billion

Business rates – £28 billion

Income tax – £170 billion

VAT – £131 billion

National Insurance – £113 billion

Corporation tax – £42 billion

Excise duties – £47 billion

Source: Office For Budget Responsibility, 2015/16 estimate (HM Treasury, 2015, p 6)

twenty-first centuries. Indeed, political campaigning has frequently focused on cutting taxes (especially income taxes) to restrict the amount of 'your money' that is taken by government, with social democratic parties, like the British Labour Party, criticised as profligate if they advocate policies to 'tax and spend'. This is reflected in popular discourses on tax – see Box 4.5.

Box 4.5 Tax payers and tax collectors

Tax payers has positive connotations associated with people contributing to the public good, and expecting governments to be accountable and responsible in their use of 'our taxes'. This is represented in the UK by organisations like The TaxPayers' Alliance, which campaigns for restrictions on levels of taxation.

Tax collectors, or the 'taxman', has negative connotations associated with public bureaucrats who are taking our money from us, and whom we are justified in seeking to avoid by organising our finances to reduce as much as possible the taxes that we pay.

However, as discussed in Chapter 7, the evidence from attitude surveys suggests that popular perceptions of taxation and public spending, and the priorities within these, are more complex than this simple aversion to payment and demand for accountability might suggest. In particular, some areas of expenditure on public welfare seem to attract more popular support then others.

This might suggest that one of the ways to make taxation and spending on welfare more popular would be to link taxation payments directly to particular areas of spending. This is what economists call *hypothecated* taxes; National Insurance (NI) contributions have been a longstanding example of this within the UK welfare system. In fact, the link between NI contributions and benefits is a complex one, but most of the expenditure does go on pensions for those who have made contributions during their working lives, and this is a link that many, especially older, contributors value. However, it is not consistently adhered to, and in 2003 the Labour government raised NI contribution rates, rather than income tax, largely because they judged that this would be a more popular tax rise, even though the expenditure raised was earmarked for spending on health and education.

Labour's move exposed some of the problems and contradictions with hypothecated taxes. It may make raising taxes for popular causes easier; but we also need to respond to less popular welfare needs, and raising taxes for these may then become even more difficult. What is more, using hypothecated taxation to meet different needs, as Labour did, will over time undermine any positive associations that these might have promoted. More generally, hypothecated taxation for all the different areas of public spending would be impractical to organise and deliver, and in any case could really only be symbolic, unless citizens were given the opportunity to opt out of those taxes that they did not like – which would be even more impractical. In any event, governments do publish information on how and where spending is made. This is summarised in the annual Budget – see Figure 4.2. Ultimately, therefore, the performance of the government in managing public expenditure could be judged from this, although in practice probably only very few people follow public expenditure planning so closely.

Figure 4.2: Public expenditure: spending 2015/16

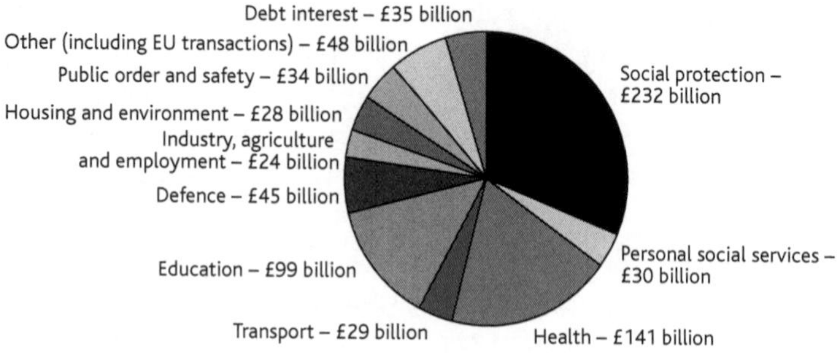

Debt interest – £35 billion
Other (including EU transactions) – £48 billion
Public order and safety – £34 billion
Housing and environment – £28 billion
Industry, agriculture and employment – £24 billion
Defence – £45 billion
Education – £99 billion
Transport – £29 billion
Social protection – £232 billion
Personal social services – £30 billion
Health – £141 billion

Source: Office For Budget Responsibility, 2015/16 estimate (HM Treasury, 2015, p 6)

Taxation is the main source of funding for collective welfare services, and it is the only one that is based on a democratic mandate through the election of governments who determine rates of taxation and spending. However, there are other sources of funding for the public provision of welfare. Commercial providers in private markets charge fees for their services, which are designed to make a profit for them and their shareholders – and which may (or may not) be covered by private insurance policies. However, as Glennerster (1997) has explained, fees and charges can also be found in public welfare services.

There have been charges for some services within the NHS, for instance, since prescription charges were introduced as early as 1951. These now only affect a minority, as explained above, but they have been joined by charges for dental and optical treatment. There are also charges for many social care services, such as home visits and residential care, and for some aspects of education, such as school meals and (most significantly perhaps, as explained in Chapter 3) university education.

Charges fulfil a number of functions in public services, as Glennerster (1997) discussed. Most obviously, they supplement the resource base, but they can also link these resources to user needs and preferences, so that for some aspects of services users only pay for what they use. In public services charges need not be geared to making a profit, and indeed can be 'subsidised' so that they only constitute a contribution to full costs. It is quite common for public service fees and charges to cover only partial costs. This can make them less daunting; where they are very small or nominal, however, they may do little more than cover the costs involved in collecting them, which is probably self-defeating. According to the Audit Commission (2013), local authorities in England raised around £10.6 billion for charges for services, about 10 per cent of their total service expenditure. This included things like car parking and leisure services, so income from welfare services was even lower, although social care charges also brought in about 10 per cent of expenditure on these.

Even small fees and charges can exclude those on low incomes who cannot afford to pay them, however. This has been recognised in many charging regimes, with means-tested (or other targeted) exemptions from charges introduced for some users. While exempting some, these add significant complexity to the administration of and access to welfare, and they extend the impact of the poverty trap discussed earlier. What is more, if they are extensive, as is the case with exemptions from NHS prescription charges in England, they may mean that in practice only a small proportion of users actually pay them. Fees and charges have never been a significant resource for public welfare, therefore, and this is likely to remain the case in the foreseeable future.

The other area of resources to pay for welfare identified by Glennerster (1997) was charitable donations. As explained above, third sector organisations have always played a significant role in the delivery of welfare services. These organisations draw on volunteer time and gifts of money or other resources, although the scale and balance of these vary enormously across different organisations. Charitable giving for public goods has been recognised in policy since the early seventeenth century, and charities are now defined and regulated by the Charities Act 2006 in England and Wales, with similar regulation in Scotland and Northern Ireland. And, as discussed above, the role of charities and other voluntary organisations in the delivery of public services is now openly supported and promoted by government.

Volunteering and charitable giving does not just take place in voluntary organisations, however. Volunteers give time to NHS and local authority health and social care services, and may also support activities in schools, most obviously through 'parent–teacher associations'. Donors also give money to public bodies; for example, most universities now actively encourage donations and legacies as key sources of income, and for some these can be substantial amounts – notably Oxford and Cambridge in the UK, which have many wealthy alumni. The role and scale of charitable funding varies across different welfare regimes and is generally much more significant in liberal regimes such as the USA, where for some of the leading universities, for example, donations and legacies are the major sources of funding. However, it is important in all, and is generally encouraged by governments.

In the UK donations to charitable organisations are exempted from income tax under a scheme called Gift Aid, which permits organisations to claim back from Her Majesty's Revenue and Customs (HMRC) the tax that has been paid by donors, assuming that they were earning enough to be paying income tax. More recently, legacy giving has also been encouraged by exemption from inheritance tax for donations in wills. The Coalition government published a White Paper outlining policies to encourage giving in 2011, including a range of measures to promote giving, such as tax exemptions and matched funding. However, significant changes in giving over time in the UK have not been great, with levels and demographic patterns remaining more or less similar over the last decade of so.

As a collective resource for welfare, therefore, there are some serious problems with charitable giving. Donations, of money or time, are voluntary. Not all people do give, and much giving is sporadic and reactive, for instance, in response to national campaigns like Children in Need. Which causes people choose to give to will also depend on their particular concerns and priorities, and these may not necessarily align well with welfare needs. For instance, some animal charities like the RSPCA are relatively popular causes for charitable donors, whereas organisations working with people with substance misuse issues, ex-offenders or asylum seekers are not. According to the annual *UK civil society almanac* produced by the NCVO (Kane et al, 2015), overseas aid and medical charities were the most popular causes, receiving 14 per cent and 13 per cent of all total donations respectively, followed by children and hospitals on 12 per cent each and animals on 11 per cent, with homelessness, disability and the elderly all receiving less than 5 per cent. Charitable giving may not be going to where it is most needed for welfare provision, therefore, and may not in practice be a consistent and reliable resource over time. What is more, the variable impact of charitable funding is compounded by the support offered through Gift Aid, which means that, indirectly, public funding through tax resources is going as an additional resource to those causes and organisations that individual donors have chosen to support.

Charitable giving and voluntary action have been an important dimension of the growth and development of collective welfare, and they continue to support important causes and promote innovative and responsive organisational development. However, they are better understood and promoted as a supplement to publicly funded services, rather than as an alternative to these. There is also the concern that, ideologically, they may contribute to some of the resistance to taxation as a resource for welfare services, by encouraging people to think that it is better to decide for themselves where 'their' money is spent, rather than leaving it to the 'bureaucrats' in government – a form of 'back door' hypothecated funding, which would not serve us well as a reliable means of paying for collective welfare.

Summary

Delivering welfare means ensuring that the resources are available to meet the needs of all citizens and that citizens are able to access this support through the services designed to provide them. This requires a redistribution of resources, and there are different models informing this redistribution and the service delivery that flows from it. Vertical redistribution and selective services move resources from 'rich' to 'poor' and target provision on those in need. However, they create a divisive culture of 'them and us', which suggests that some only benefit, while others only pay. In reality this is not the case for many welfare services; horizontal redistribution and universal access to services remain important features of welfare provision in the UK, and in most other welfare regimes, and they can underpin a stronger collective interest in investment in public services.

However they are funded, welfare services need to be accessible to, and taken up by, their potential users. This has created a challenge to the 'provider culture' of much of the post-war welfare state, and it has led to a range of measures to seek to improve the delivery and responsiveness of welfare services. There is a tension here between the 'top down' accountability of management practices and the 'bottom up' empowerment of welfare users. It is important to ensure that users are involved in the production and delivery of the services from which they benefit. This cannot be achieved simply by introducing market competition, however, because in many of the most important public services commercial markets cannot operate.

We must also pay for these welfare services, and, although fees and charges and charitable giving can make a contribution to meeting the costs of welfare, these are not as effective and reliable as the main sources of income for public services. We need taxation to finance the investment we must make in public welfare, and securing support for taxation and public investment remains at the heart of the challenge of delivering welfare.

Key texts

Hills' (2015) book on the distributional implications of welfare policy is the best and most comprehensive guide to some of the complex, but important, issues involved. Deakin and Wright's (1990) collection of papers provides a useful guide to some of the problems with the provider culture, which are still relevant today. Discussion of the issues involved in producing and delivering welfare has been taken up by Butcher (2002) and Miller (2004). Le Grand's (2003) book on motivation and agency is the most important contribution to understanding why agency matters in welfare delivery. Flynn (2012) is the best textbook on new public management, and Boyle's (2001) attack on target setting is the most accessible critique of one of its key features. Needham and Glasby (2014) is a topical guide to some of the issues involved in the recent moves to promote personalisation and co-production. Glennerster (1997) remains a good introduction to the different ways in which welfare is funded, and his more recent book on the financing of welfare (Glennerster, 2009) examines the arguments behind public funding and the ways in which different services are financed.

5

Where should planning and delivery take place?

Where we live matters to us. To a significant extent, it determines the social context and social relations within which we operate as social beings. It also matters for the delivery of welfare. When collective resources have to be collected and distributed, who should be included in this? And how far does our collective responsibility extend? How *far* collective responsibility extends is a matter of geography, and the geographical, or spatial, dimensions of welfare provision are critical to understanding how it is organised and, more importantly, to making the case for how and why it should be organised. However, the geographical dimensions of welfare are more complex than we might at first expect. They raise difficult questions about what is the appropriate spatial level for policy planning; as I discuss in this chapter, there are no simple answers to these questions.

National government

We all live in nation states, governed by national governments, which, in democratic countries, we elect and can change, usually within fixed periods of time. Much of social policy is developed and implemented at national government level. When we talk about the welfare state, we are generally referring to the policies and practices of national governments; as mentioned in Chapter 1, the 'creation' of the British welfare state by the post-war Labour government in the 1940s was very much a process of national policy making.

However, policy making does not only take place at national level – nor does the delivery of public services, even when they are developed nationally. The post-war British welfare state may have been the 'high water mark' of national planning in this country, but even within this, significant roles were retained and created for local government. In fact, much of UK welfare provision was initially developed by local government (see Alcock with May, 2014, Ch 6), and, despite some centralisation, much has remained in local hands. Furthermore, in the last two decades there have been some significant moves to further 'localise' welfare provision, as well as others aspects of public planning.

Nevertheless, at least since the reforms of the post-war period, national planning for welfare has been at the centre of UK policy making. However, within the UK the national base for policy planning is in fact rather complex. The post-war welfare state was created by a UK government, based at the national Parliament in Westminster, and policies were developed for the whole of the UK. However, the United Kingdom, as the name suggests, is in fact a unity of partially separate nations. There are England, Scotland and Wales, which together make up Britain, and, since the creation of the Irish Republic in the early twentieth century, there is also Northern Ireland, which is geographically part of Ireland but politically part of the UK.

There have always been some differences between these different nations (or sub-nations) within the UK. For instance, Scotland has always had a separate and different legal system, and in many parts of Wales a different language (Welsh) is spoken. However, the differences between these UK nations has become much more significant, especially for social policy purposes, since the devolution of some political powers and policy making to the new elected parliaments and assemblies in Scotland, Wales and Northern Ireland in 1999.

A number of important areas of welfare policy have been devolved, including education, health and social care, although not social security. This has led to some significant, and increasing, differences in policy. As mentioned in Chapter 3, all the devolved administrations have abolished prescriptions charges within their now separate NHSs. For example, the NHS here is now

NHSE (England), with separate services in Scotland, Wales and Northern Ireland. Scotland has also introduced free social care for people with long-term sickness or disability. In Scotland, Wales and Northern Ireland tuition fees are not charged to university students from those countries, although the arrangements in each are different, with Scotland being the most generous to students. More generally, there is much less commitment to the contracting out and marketisation of public services like the NHS in all three devolved administrations than is the case in England, and overall levels of public spending are higher.

As a result of this, many of the policy issues and dilemmas that commentators and academics discuss in the UK are actually policy issues for England only – although with 84 per cent (53 million) of the 63 million people in the UK living in England, these apply to the largest proportion of the population. In 2014 a referendum was held in Scotland on the question of whether the country should leave the UK and become an independent country. A significant majority (55 per cent) voted against this. However, the active campaigning on the question led to commitments from the Westminster government to further devolution of economic and social policy making to Scotland. And these pressures for further devolution have been accentuated since the Scottish Nationalist Party won almost all of the Scottish seats in the 2015 election and became the third largest party at Westminster.

The shared legacy of almost two centuries of UK policy making, however, including in particular the public welfare policies of the twentieth century, means that, despite devolution, much of national welfare provision remains the same across the UK. But with different political parties in power within the devolved parliaments and assemblies, differences are beginning to grow in the new century – with the result that the national politics of welfare in the UK is now increasingly fragmented – although whether and how these differences will be likely to benefit UK citizens remains controversial, and may depend in part upon where those citizens live. Even at national level in the UK now, geography matters.

Local government

The creation of the post-war welfare state was, as I have suggested, arguably the high water mark of national policy making in the UK. And this was a time when national welfare policy development was taking place in most other advanced industrial nations too. Glennerster captures this national fervour for central control in this quote from the beginning of his book on the history of post-war welfare in the UK:

> To make these goals a reality the central state took on clear responsibilities for the key areas of social policy: social security, health, education, and housing to a lesser extent. Local authorities in these respects became agents of a central government while retaining initiative and independence over detail. (2007, p 7)

Some of the post-war welfare policies were therefore moves to nationalise welfare provision which had been developed earlier in the century and before by local government. The creation of the NHS involved the nationalisation of local authority healthcare and local and voluntary hospitals. The Butler Education Act of 1944 provided a broad national framework for primary and secondary education, which had been developed and delivered by local government.

The welfare policies of the mid twentieth century were therefore something of a centralisation of public provision, which had previously been controlled and developed by local government. Part of the reasoning behind this was a concern to ensure consistency and efficiency in service delivery and to ensure that minimum standards could be guaranteed for all, so that whatever the social, economic or political situation locally, all citizens would have the same access to the same welfare services. This was a challenge to what has subsequently come to be referred to as the 'postcode lottery', where local differences can lead to better, or worse, services for citizens who have the same needs, but happen to be living in different areas.

In practice, however, the centralisation of the post-war UK welfare state was always only partial. Education, social care and housing remained the responsibility of local government; and as these services expanded in the latter half of the last century, so did public spending on them and the power of local government to control this. What is more, when in the 1980s a Conservative central government wanted to contain public spending, this led them into conflict with (mainly Labour) local authorities who wished to protect or even expand their local welfare services. The political conflict between Labour local authorities, in places like Sheffield and Greater London, and the Conservative central government brought into sharp relief the politics of local versus central control of welfare. However, it was a conflict which, with its greater powers, central government was bound to win. By the end of the 1980s national controls had been introduced over local government spending, and some authorities, notably the Greater London Council (GLC), had been abolished altogether.

Whatever this meant for services, both locally and nationally, it was in effect yet a further move towards the centralisation of politics and policy making in the country. It meant that the UK became more firmly established as one of the most centralised welfare regimes. For instance, in the US, Australia, Germany and France, local state administrations have much greater political autonomy and policy making responsibility than do local authorities in the UK. Centralisation means consistency in public services – no postcode lotteries – but it can also mean conformity, and in the late twentieth and early twenty-first centuries this began to come under challenge from critics of the supposedly monopolistic and bureaucratic tendencies of central public services.

In fact, however, all services involve some mixture of central and local control over planning and delivery. Even national services like the NHS and social security benefits need to be administered locally by clinical commissioning groups and jobcentres, and a balance between central administration and local delivery is a feature of all welfare services. What is more, these different welfare services are being used (or perhaps not) by local people who will frequently need to access more than one to meet their needs. This is most obviously the case in social care, where central health service planning interacts with local authority care services – but perhaps does not interact effectively, as is revealed in the problem of 'bed-blocking' (people with disabilities or long-term sickness being kept in hospital beds, even though there is no real treatment being provided, as there are no places in local residential or nursing homes for them to move into).

It is increasingly recognised that there is a need for the local delivery of services to be more 'joined-up' – a phrase popularised by the Labour government of the 2000s. And in recent years attempts to join up service delivery have been pursued, in particular in greater joint planning of health and social care, but also in other areas such as children's services and employment support. The local coordination of public services has also led to debate about how this might involve a move from the local *government* of services to an alternative model of local *governance*. This is part of a more general shift in public policy, which is taking place at national level too and is linked to the role of alternative providers of services discussed in Chapter 4 (see Newman, 2001). While government implies the 'command and control' of services by politicians and government officers, governance is more of a coordinating role where local authorities (or national governments) are only one party among a collection of agencies (including private companies and third sector representatives) acting together to plan and deliver services. The role of local government here thus becomes one of *enabling* service provision, rather than delivering services – sometimes also referred to as a shift from 'rowing to steering' (Clarke and Stewart, 1988).

Improved local planning of services implies a more general debate, of course, as to what is the most appropriate (perhaps most efficient and most effective) balance between central and local control over welfare. After a century of centralisation in the UK, some recent governments have become keen to promote a shift (back?) to a greater degree of local control over public services – referred to by the Coalition government in the early 2010s as a policy of 'localisation'. This raises the further question, however, of just what we mean by local. In practice this is more complex, and controversial, than just greater powers and resources (or not) for local government.

The Labour governments of the 2000s sought to develop a new level of regional governance for some aspects of social and economic planning, in recognition of the fact that for some important aspects of economic and social development, existing local government boundaries may be too small and exclusive. This is most obviously the case in London, where the abolition of the GLC in the 1980s led eventually to a return to regional planning across the capital with the creation in 2000 of an elected London Assembly and office of the Mayor of London – first held by Ken Livingstone, the former leader of the GLC.

Outside of London, however, after 2010 the Coalition government largely dropped Labour's plans for regional government in England (the devolved administrations in Scotland, Wales and Northern Ireland are in effect a form of regional government there in any case). They were keener, they said, to promote instead a greater devolution of powers below local government to neighbourhoods and communities, sometimes referred to as *double devolution* (Mulgan and Bury, 2006). The Localism Act of 2011 freed up local authorities to undertake any task not specifically prohibited by legislation. It also gave local communities new powers over local planning, and the right to purchase local assets and challenge local authority delivery of public services.

Despite the new concern for double devolution, however, the scope for larger regional planning to replace some aspects of both local and national policy development and delivery has not disappeared, and has been taken up again in the late 2010s in the devolution of large chunks of public service budgets (including health and education) to the 'city region' of Greater Manchester, in an attempt, once again, to promote greater joining-up of services here; similar moves are likely to follow for other major cities. This has been largely welcomed, in particular by local politicians, who see in the shift of resources and planning from Westminster to Manchester a potential revitalisation of the kind of municipal development that led to the initial creation of many public services, notably in cities like Birmingham, at the beginning of the last century (Stoker, 1991). The local scale for policy planning is thus getting bigger, at the same time as it is supposed to be getting smaller too.

Neighbourhoods and communities

Double devolution was promoted because of a belief by government that even local government control does not move decisions over the planning and delivery of welfare services close enough to the citizens and communities who use and benefit from them. In fact, the spatial scale of local government in the UK varies significantly, and is complicated by the continued split in most rural areas between county and district councils, with the larger county councils controlling education and social care, and the smaller district councils controlling infrastructure like transport and housing. In urban areas there is normally only one authority, although even these can be quite large. For instance, Birmingham City Council, the largest, has a population of over a million, larger than some small countries.

It may be difficult for big local authorities like Birmingham to engage directly with citizens across what is also a very diverse city, economically and ethnically. The idea behind double devolution, therefore, is for councils to transfer control over services and resources to smaller neighbourhood or community forums, where local citizens can participate directly in decisions on how these should be organised and delivered. Behind this is a belief that such 'associative' (or deliberative) democracy (Hirst, 1994; see also Stoker, 2006) will involve people more closely in the design and delivery of welfare, empowering them and giving them 'ownership' of the services that they have had a hand in developing. At the same time, it is argued, such local engagement will also improve the relevance and responsiveness of services to local needs. In this sense, therefore, double devolution has the potential to produce what some pundits call a 'win/win' situation.

However, even here some of the practical problems of spatial planning remain. For a start, what constitutes a neighbourhood? Most local authorities are broken down into smaller 'wards', represented by one or two councillors. But these may not be experienced as neighbourhoods by the people living in them; indeed, they are likely to be too large for people to know many of their 'neighbours' within them.

References to communities are even more controversial: there is an extensive theoretical debate about what may or may not constitute a community (see Taylor, 2011, especially Ch 4). For instance, geographical communities (which may be much the same thing as neighbourhoods) are contrasted with 'communities of interest', such as ethnic or migrant groups, religious sects or congregations, or any group of citizens sharing a collective interest or commitment. Both are arguably communities, but they are very different in form and activity, and involving them in service planning would require very different strategies for engagement.

There have also been a range of policy and practice initiatives to support or develop communities, including the government-sponsored Community Development Projects (CDPs) in the 1960s and 1970s and the New Deal for Communities (NDC) in the 2000s. Similar initiatives have been undertaken too in most other welfare regimes; indeed, the CDPs in the UK were largely modelled on earlier programmes for local community development established in the US in the early 1960s (Alcock, 2006, Ch 15). There is also an extensive academic literature seeking to explain and explore different strategies for community development (see Taylor, 2011), including an international *Community Development Journal*.

The notion of community is therefore difficult to pin down. While many policy planners may want to respond to or promote community engagement in policy development and delivery, it is never entirely clear what is meant by this. What is more, even if we could arrive at some agreement on what is meant by neighbourhood and community devolution, this would not in any event avoid the problems of the postcode lottery, and the potential for inequity, and inefficiency, in service provision. Indeed, devolving resources and decision making to small groups of local citizens could lead to significant disparities in both engagement with the process of community planning and the policy outcomes of this. It is likely, too, that these disparities would reflect broader social and economic inequalities in the distribution of power and resources, with higher levels of engagement in wealthier middle class communities, where needs are arguably less acute, and lower levels of engagement and potentially poorer service outcomes in deprived neighbourhoods where problems are greater.

Localisation and community engagement can take service planning and delivery closer to the geographical and community places in which people live, and, potentially at least, involve them more directly in service planning. Whether that leads to better services for all, however, is far from certain.

Supra-national policy planning

Challenges to the national planning of welfare policy in recent decades have not just come from 'below', through localisation. They have also come from 'above', through what commentators have referred to as *globalisation* (Mishra, 1999). There have always been international influences on policy making in different nation states, but with the increasing pace and impact of international travel and information technology since the latter part of the last century, these have become more extensive, and more pervasive. For example, we can now travel within the European continent in a few hours, and to the other side of the world in a day – and our leading politicians frequently do. Additionally, at the click of a mouse we can read research evidence and analysis from around the world, and find out what policy differences exist in a wide range of different welfare regimes.

Knowledge of international variation in policy practice makes it easier for politicians and policy makers to engage in what political scientists call 'policy transfer'. That is, taking ideas from policies that have worked (or not) in other countries and implementing them in others. For instance, in the UK the New Deal and Working Tax Credits, introduced by the Labour governments between 1997 and 2010, owed much to the earlier welfare reforms implemented by the Clinton administration in the US (Dolowitz, 1998). However, international influences now extend beyond voluntary transfer or comparative policy analysis, to the direct involvement of supra-national agencies in policy making in different nation states.

In the UK this is most obviously the case as a result of our membership of the European Union (EU). This means that policies developed at EU level by the EU Commission generally apply across all member states. This has resulted in changes in UK policy in areas such as employment rights and local economic development. Although there has been some opposition in the UK to the 'imposition' of policies on the country by 'bureaucrats in Brussels', in general, EU policy making has strengthened collective welfare provision in all member states and extended the range and depth of the 'social rights' identified by Marshall (1950) discussed in Chapter 2. Unless Britain were to leave the EU, the Commission's influence on national policy making will likely continue, or increase.

The EU is a membership organisation based in Europe. There are other international organisations which operate on a broader international basis reaching, potentially at least, right across the globe. These include the United Nations (UN) and its subsidiary agencies, such as the United Nations Development Programme (UNDP), the United Nations Children's Fund (UNICEF), the World Health Organization (WHO) and the International Labour Organisation (ILO), which gather research evidence and promote policy development on an international basis. They also include powerful economic agencies like the International Monetary Fund (IMF) and the World Bank.

The IMF has the power to require countries to make policy changes or meet agreed targets in return for international financial support at times of national economic need, as has happened at times in the UK, most notably during the economic recession of the 1970s, when the IMF required public spending targets to be reduced (see Alcock with May, 2014, Ch 15). The World Bank has promoted a range of economic and social policy measures in countries around the world, again often linked to external international support for national or local policy development.

These major global policy actors have become an important influence on national policy making across the world, especially in developing welfare regimes in the global South, as Deacon (2007) and Yeates (2008) have discussed. They are a clear example of the globalisation of policy making, although, as critics like Deacon and Yeates also argue, there is no consensus on whether this is always a good thing for all countries – for a Western, neoliberal model of welfare policy has often dominated the practices of agencies like the IMF and the World Bank.

What this reveals, therefore, is that in the twenty-first century welfare policy making is less of a national affair than it was for much of the early part of the twentieth century. This has led some commentators to refer to the dual influences of globalisation and localisation as resulting in a 'hollowing out' of the national welfare state (Newman, 2001). This has certainly been happening in the UK. What is more difficult to judge, is whether this hollowing out has been a good or a bad thing for the development of collective welfare.

Equity and national planning

The hollowing out of the nation state provides a challenge to the supporters of the national public services of the twentieth-century welfare state. Do the increasing trends towards localisation and globalisation mean that national planning should no longer be at the heart of the collective provision of welfare? Are decisions over the collection and distribution of resources and access to services best taken by smaller groups of people in local neighbourhoods and communities? Are supra-national organisations and agencies now more powerful than nation states? Important and far-reaching though some of these challenges to national policy making have become over recent decades, they have not replaced the central role that national policy making must play in the collective provision of welfare.

At the broader political level, in a democracy like the UK, as in most other Western welfare regimes, it is only national governments that have a mandate to act on behalf of all citizens. Local governments are also elected, but their powers are constrained by central government. Local authorities in the UK have very limited tax raising powers – Council Tax contributes less than 15 per cent of the income of most councils, with the vast majority, over 75 per cent, of the resources spent locally coming from central government grants. And, as mentioned above, only a limited number of services are actually devolved to local authorities to administer. Also, the scale and structure of local government in the country varies dramatically. It does not, as explained below, provide a rational basis for collective welfare planning.

This political mandate means that national government collects taxes from all citizens (or at least all those who should be paying these). It passes legislation to implement the policies discussed and agreed in Parliament. Through its civil servants and national public agencies it plans service provision, and, except where this has been devolved to local government, it delivers benefits and services to citizens. It is no coincidence, therefore, that the most important period of collective welfare reform in the UK, the creation of the post-war welfare state, was a period of national policy making, including, as explained above, the nationalisation of a number of previously local services.

It was the belief of the post-war Labour government that only nationally planned services could guarantee consistency of provision for all citizens. In particular, this was because collective redistribution (both horizontal and vertical) could compensate for pre-existing disparities in social and economic conditions, including those between different geographical areas. Such redistribution is legitimate because it is carried out by national governments, who are accountable to all citizens; despite the difficulties in securing support for taxation to pay for services, few would deny that taxation (or *fiscal policy* as this aspect of government activity is called) is a critical feature of the role of central government. Indeed, it is frequently the most important issue raised in campaigning for general elections.

At a practical level too national planning is important. Economies of scale and greater efficiency in resource planning can be achieved at national level. It would be quite counter-productive to duplicate across a range of local settings the regulation and fiscal planning that underpins most service development. National standards mean the services are consistent across different geographical places, so that when people move from place to place (as many of course do over the course of their lives) their current needs and future expectations will be met to the same extent, and so that wherever people live these needs and expectations will be treated equally. National services are also easier to understand and promote, since the same information and processes apply to all. This was a critical feature of the early years of the post-war welfare state, when national advertising was used to promote the new services to citizens, who it was concerned would not immediately grasp that everyone now had the same social rights.

It is essential, therefore, that national welfare services remain the core basis for collective welfare provision. We must continue to promote the social rights of all citizens, as well as the responsibility that they also have to contribute to the services they need or will come to need at some point in their lives.

National welfare in the UK is complicated now by the devolution of politics and policy making to the separate administrations in Scotland, Wales and Northern Ireland, however. As explained above, a number of key areas of welfare policy have now been devolved, with differences in national planning beginning to become more significant. However, it is important to remember that for the most part it is the internal structure and delivery of services that have been devolved to the new administrations. Overall decision making on redistribution, and in particular fiscal policy, is still determined at UK level. This redistribution in fact currently favours the citizens of Scotland, Wales and Northern Ireland because since the 1970s it has been determined by something called the Barnett formula – see Box 5.1.

Box 5.1 The Barnett formula

This is an aspect of UK fiscal policy designed to set the levels of public spending in the separate nations of Scotland, Wales and Northern Ireland. It is named after the Labour government Treasury Minister, Joel Barnett, who devised it in the late 1970s. One of the most important consequences of the formula is that public spending levels have become higher in Scotland, Wales and Northern Ireland, with all of these countries having higher levels of per capita spending (around 20 per cent higher) than England, the highest being Northern Ireland and the lowest (apart from England) being Wales.

There is an established process of redistribution of resources going on at this national level within the UK, and although some UK governments have threatened to review or remove the Barnett formula, so far none have. The Scottish independence referendum of 2014 was based upon a bid to secure complete control over all taxes and spending for an independent Scotland. In practice, though, it was not clear to all Scottish citizens what might be the outcome of this, in particular, perhaps, because much of the case for independence was based on the value that the country could then extract from its North Sea oil reserves, which at the time were declining in value as the price of oil on international markets was falling rapidly.

Despite losing the independence referendum the Scottish Nationalist Party have continued to campaign for fiscal autonomy for Scotland, and will press the Westminster government on this following the 2015 election. However, this would mean the loss of the benefits that the country currently gains from the Barnett formula, and according to analysis by the Institute for Fiscal Studies (IFS) could leave a significant 'hole' in the resources for welfare services in Scotland. In this context, greater fiscal autonomy for the devolved administrations to pursue separate national policy planning could be something of a mixed blessing for the citizens of these countries.

Subsidiarity and local autonomy

If we conclude that national policy making will need to remain at the centre of collective planning and investment in welfare provision, then this raises a question about whether there is a role for local involvement in provision of public services. Part of the problem here is the current structure of local government in the UK. It is probably fair to say that, if we were now to begin planning a structure for local government in the country, we would not arrive at the arrangements we currently have. They are a product of history, and of a series of political shifts and compromises over time – for example, the abolition of the GLC and large metropolitan councils in the 1980s when these had come into conflict with the central government of the time. What we have is not a logical structure, nor in practice an equitable one, with the largest councils (notably Birmingham with its one million population) having access to large budgets, but also facing massive demands for services, and some small rural district councils administering only a few services to a small local population (some of the smallest serving only around 50,000).

Recent moves to promote localisation have extended the powers of local authorities to take on new tasks, at least in theory. But in practice, with much reduced resources as a result of expenditure cutbacks, most are unlikely to be expanding their range of activities – and indeed are more likely to be cutting back commitments as far as possible. In any event, localisation does not address the unequal scale and responsibilities of authorities or the implications of their different political control for local public services. The problem of the postcode lottery still remains therefore.

Nevertheless, most welfare services need to be delivered locally to citizens and communities, and so some provision must be made for local organisation and access. What is more, this needs to address the challenge of 'joining-up' the planning and delivery of different services, such as health and social care. The Greater Manchester city region devolution is a relatively new, and radical, departure in such local (or regional) planning. It has the capacity to herald a new basis for the local coordination of services at a scale that existing local authorities could not achieve. However, even this is best seen as the development of a different scale for the local planning and delivery of national services, rather than a substitute for, or replacement of, national collective investment and policy making.

The same is largely true for neighbourhood and community 'double devolution'. It is undoubtedly the case that such localised engagement will be likely to promote associative democracy and empower local citizens and communities. Furthermore, local involvement in service planning and delivery is likely to increase the commitment of citizens to such collective investment; in this sense, it is a 'win/win' development.

However, it is because such localisation is a *process* of engagement and empowerment that it cannot provide a secure and consistent basis for broader collective planning. Local citizens and communities can, and should, have some control over the detailed features of local services, such as opening times, staff recruitment or local priority setting. But our collective interest in the common good is essentially a national, not a local, investment, and this cannot just be passed down to local communities, who may be quite unprepared or unable to take on responsibility for anything beyond low level local priority setting.

The need for national policy planning is based on the importance of equity and consistency in service provision, and recognition of what it means to invest in the common good. But this does not mean that some aspects of organisation and delivery cannot be devolved to more local levels. In this context, the EU has developed the use of a principle called *subsidiarity*, which has a longer history of usage in a number of continental European countries, such as Germany. The principle of subsidiarity is that, wherever possible, decisions should be taken at the closest effective local basis. This is only a principle, however; the question is, what does it mean in practice? Within the EU subsidiarity has now come to mean a restriction on the role of EU-wide law and policy making to situations where it is judged that member states cannot act individually – see Box 5.2.

Box 5.2 Subsidiarity and the EU

Subsidiarity was established by the EU in the Maastricht Treaty of 1993. It was reformulated in 2009 and is currently contained in Article 5(3) of the Treaty of the European Union, following the Lisbon Treaty, which states that:

> Under the principle of subsidiarity, in areas which do not fall within its exclusive competence, the Union shall act only if and in so far as the objectives of the proposed action cannot be sufficiently achieved by the Member States, either at central level or at regional and local level, but can rather, by reason of the scale or effects of the proposed action, be better achieved at Union level.

This is a rather restrictive interpretation of the broader principle of subsidiarity on which the EU treaty makers drew, and in practice within the Union it has mainly been used by member states to curb what they see as the excesses of EU Commission interference with national politics and policy making. Nevertheless, as a principle, it does provide a good basis for beginning a consideration about what might be the most appropriate level for spatial planning. The question we should always being asking, it implies, is how far can decision making be devolved? Nevertheless, as with here in the EU, the default position for responsibility should always be the national state.

In this sense, therefore, the subsidiarity principle applies to assessment of the value of global action too. There are advantages to supra-national policy action. Within the EU it has worked to ensure consistent practices across member states, where internal competition could have been potentially damaging. EU legislation on employment rights has restricted the scope for dysfunctional trends like *social dumping* (where employers seek to locate activities in those countries where workers' rights and benefits costs are lowest) and *social tourism* (where workers seek to move to those countries where rights and benefits are highest). However, the EU remains in essence a membership club for nations, and they must retain national control over all major aspects of social and economic policy – unless (or until) the Union becomes one massive European nation state.

Such limited broader coordination is also likely to be the best role for the other international agencies mentioned above. The UN can promote international and comparative social development, especially through its agencies like the WHO, promoting improved health outcomes across the world, but this remains predominantly a communication and promotional role. The IMF and the World Bank can act to support, or even command, national and local development through the targeted use of collective international resources. But this is a supplementary role to national policy making, and it is best used to promote and assist effective (and autonomous) national governments, rather than to impose the Western neoliberal models of policy making that have sometimes dominated the work of these agencies.

Summary

Where we live matters, and in the context of welfare it can determine the services we receive or are entitled to, particularly from public agencies. Where welfare policy is planned and delivered is therefore important in determining how it operates. Within this, a range of different spatial levels of engagement have different roles to play. There is a role for citizen engagement with policy planning and delivery at community and neighbourhood levels, and there is a role for local and regional planning to ensure that services are 'joined-up' across large areas like Greater Manchester. There is also a role for supra-national agencies. Membership clubs, like the EU, can regulate to ensure consistency in welfare provision across member nations, and major international agencies like the UN and the World Bank can influence and support welfare planning in different national settings right across the world. Part of the challenge for the planning and delivery of welfare services is to get this balance of spatial aggregation and devolution right – to ensure that *equity* can coexist with *subsidiarity*. We need to be wary of both the 'postcode lottery' and the ideological pressures created by powerful global agencies – and in particular we need to be wary of the 'hollowing out' of the national welfare state. For it is the national welfare state that remains at the centre of this balance. It is national welfare planning that will continue to provide the only effective and legitimate basis for the collective investment and distribution that the public provision of welfare requires.

Key texts

Glennerster (2007) and Timmins (2001) provide good historical accounts of the creation and development of the post-war British welfare state. Lodge and Schmuecker (2010) is a collection of papers on the impact of national devolution within the UK on social policy. Stoker (1991) is the best book on the history and politics of local government, and his more recent text on *Why politics matters* (Stoker, 2006) is an excellent analysis of how, where and why decision making takes place, including discussion of associative democracy. Taylor (2011) is a good discussion of the community dimensions of public policy. Hantrais (2007) provides a useful guide to the structure and practices of the EU. Deacon (2007) and Yeates (2008) are the leading authors on the role of global agencies in international policy making.

6

Who benefits from welfare?

Collective provision of welfare is based on principles of investment and inclusion. We all contribute and we all benefit. As the creators of the post-war welfare state were keen to ensure, we should all in principle have equal access to benefits and services. To employ recent political jargon, we are 'all in it together'. Implied in this is the assumption that we all have the same welfare needs and experience these needs in the same social circumstances. However, in practice, in modern societies like the UK our needs may not all be shared and the circumstances in which we experience them may not all be the same. We live in a society comprised of a range of social groups, who are divided by a series of social, economic and cultural factors. These divisions may mean that for some it does not feel at all as though we are all in things together; this applies to needs for and experiences of welfare too.

All societies are comprised of different social groups, and all experience division and sometimes conflict to some extent. These differences are extensive and multifaceted, driven by differences of gender, ethnicity, age, ability, sexuality, religion, politics, culture, geography and, of course, economic circumstances. In one sense, therefore, it may seem impossible to consider us all having any common collective experiences or interests. However, as I outlined in Chapter 2, people like Doyal and Gough (1991) and Sen (2009) have argued that there are universal human needs which we all share, whatever our social circumstances, and therefore that a relativist approach, which suggests that ultimately society is just a collection of different and disparate circumstances and experiences, fails to capture the collective nature of human social relations.

I share with Doyal and Gough, and Sen and others, an inclusive and positivist view of human society. We all do have a range of shared interests and investments based on our status as social beings, and our daily lives and future expectations depend on our active participation in social relations and our membership of a larger society. In the context of collective welfare, this means participation in a national welfare state, as explained in Chapter 5.

Nevertheless, this does not mean that we should overlook the impact of social divisions on the need for and experience of welfare. In particular, there are some key social divisions that have had a significant effect on welfare needs and service use. Social policy analysts have recognised these and policy makers have taken some steps to respond to them – although whether these have all been effective, or sufficient, remains controversial.

Age and life course

Age differences do not divide us as individuals from other citizens, of course, because at different stages of our life course we will pass through all age groups – or at least will hope to. However, at any particular point in time, age differences do lead to differences in our needs and experiences, and to a significant extent, our social circumstances too. Young and old people may sometimes feel as though they live in different worlds. Social policy has for some time sought to respond to these differences in the needs and circumstances of different age groups, in particular, through the horizontal redistribution discussed in Chapter 4. This has been aimed primarily at focusing services and benefits on children and older people.

When we are children we need the care and support of our parents or guardians, and there are a range of benefits and services to support parents in this, including in particular Child Benefit and Child Tax Allowances to supplement family income. There are also services to monitor whether children are being appropriately cared for and to intervene where neglect or abuse occurs – although these are not always effective, as a series of child abuse scandals has revealed. Furthermore, generic services like education ensure that we all reach adulthood with a range of knowledge and skills to help us to participate, and to flourish, in human social relations. Horizontal redistribution helps to focus public welfare services on children.

The other major area of age-related policy intervention is for older people, in particular, through the provision of pensions for those who have retired from employment. Pensions are the largest part of horizontal social security benefit redistribution, and they are also an increasing feature of private investment in future welfare needs. For some older people, too, there are health and social care services, where age or infirmity lead to people developing needs for personal care and support – although here much provision is privately provided by commercial or third sector agencies, for example, in nursing or residential homes, which charge fees to residents.

Children and older people remain the main foci for collective welfare provision, although age differences throughout our life course can also lead to other changes in our needs for welfare protection, notably when adults become parents and acquire direct responsibilities for another generation. However, it is the changing balance between children, adults and older people that has become of most concern more recently to policy makers in the UK, and across most other welfare regimes. In particular, here it is the growing proportion of the population who are over pension age which is seen as the most pressing issue. This is a product of greater longevity, but also in many countries of a decline in fertility in younger generations.

Average life expectancy grew throughout the twentieth century, as a result of a range of factors including improved medical treatment, public health and diet, and a safer environment for work and home life. Most adults and children can now expect to live into their 80s, with a growing minority reaching their 90s and even passing 100 years. This is largely to be welcomed, of course. However, as discussed in more detail in Chapter 7, it means a changing balance in the population between those over pension age and those below (see Figure 7.1). With people reaching pension entitlement in their mid or late 60s, and most retiring then or earlier, the cost of redistribution to older generations is growing. Also, although many (especially the 'younger old') will live happy and active lives, some (especially the 'older old') may need significant care and support. Overall, therefore, the demand for benefits and services for older people is likely to continue growing – for instance, expenditure on state pensions, which is over 65 per cent of social security spending, and on healthcare, with NHS spending on pensioner households roughly twice that on those of working age.

Whatever changes are taking place in the balance between age groups within the population, however, our collective commitment to redistribution across the life course draws largely on our shared self-interest here. We all have, and will, benefit from this redistribution, and will expect our changing needs in older age to be met, which is not the case for some of the other social divisions I discuss later. These benefits can be complicated by the cohort effects of being younger or older at different periods of broader social and economic development, as discussed in Chapter 4. Nevertheless, this shared self-interest must drive a collective trust in the belief that different generations will react similarly to the needs and demands of life course redistribution. We need our children's commitments to this now – and they need to believe that their children will share this commitment in the future. In this sense, our collective investment in the welfare for all is a long-term game, as is further discussed in Chapter 8.

Class

What we mean by social class has always been at the centre of social science debate and research. It has been the focus of theoretical debate, by theorists such as Marx and Weber, and empirical research on labour markets, the distribution of income and wealth, and social mobility – sometimes generically referred to as social stratification research. As a result, in part, of these debates, what we mean by class is controversial and contested. We talk about the working class and the middle class, and perhaps the upper class. But who is included in each category is far from settled. For instance, are teachers, nurses and doctors working class (they all work), or middle class (some, though not all, are comfortably off)? Is class a function of the job we do or our role in society, or of our economic circumstances? For instance, some workers (in information technology or financial services) will earn much more than some people who own and run their own small businesses.

The Office for National Statistics (ONS) provide a classification of social classes, based on a hierarchy of employment types, which is widely used by academics and policy makers (see Figure 6.1); and Crompton (2008) and Roberts (2011) provide useful guides to recent debates on the definition and measurement of class membership and size. As Crompton points out, however, the boundaries between classes are also changing, with the numbers of manual and skilled jobs declining over several decades (with many of these now transferred overseas), and the numbers of administrative and professional jobs growing – see Box 6.1.

Figure 6.1 The ONS socioeconomic classification

1	Higher managerial and professional occupations	
	1.1	Large employers and higher managerial occupations
	1.2	Higher professional occupations
2	Lower managerial and professional occupations	
3	Intermediate occupations	
4	Small employers and own account workers	
5	Lower supervisory and technical occupations	
6	Semi-routine occupations	
7	Routine occupations	
8	Never worked and long-term unemployed	

Source: ONS (2012)

Box 6.1 Complex class boundaries

Take the example of Sally, a state primary school teacher earning £23,000 a year, less than the national average salary in the UK in the mid-2010s. Her parents are well-off and paid for her to attend a private school. Based on her income she might be regarded as working class, but her social background and cultural experience may mean that she identifies more with middle class values. She does not have any management responsibility, but she does have a professional qualification. This would place her in class 3 or even class 2 in the ONS classification in Figure 6.1. Deciding what class she is in is therefore not clear-cut.

What matters for social policy, however, is whether the needs and circumstances of different social classes lead to different needs for, or contribution to, welfare. As discussed in Chapter 4, and as Hills (2015) explains, much of the redistribution carried out under welfare policy is designed to reduce economic differentials between citizens in different classes, through vertical redistribution and the provision of universal services – the 'social wage'. Education and health promotion policies also promote social mobility, helping to ensure that, whatever our backgrounds or circumstances, we should all be able to participate, and even flourish, in social relations.

Public welfare services are therefore largely based on the premise that social class should not determine service access or outcomes. Le Grand (1982) once argued that the articulate middle classes were better at securing preferential access to supposedly universal services like education and health, but Hills' (2015) more recent empirical analysis of the distribution of welfare revealed that overall it had led to reductions in inequality across the social spectrum, especially when use of services like education and health were taken into account.

This is not true of access to private welfare services, however. Private education and private healthcare, although only purchased by a minority, are almost exclusively the preserve of the better-off, comfortable middle classes – indeed, largely those in the top 10 per cent of the income distribution. Where these private services confer privileges and advantages, they can also reduce the scope for social mobility between classes. For instance, experience of private education is linked to higher proportions of university admissions (especially to prestigious universities) and better paid and more influential employment, and political influence – most of the members of the Coalition and Conservative governments' Cabinets attended private schools.

Private pensions also benefit better-off middle class employees, as they are more likely to be members of such schemes, and their higher salaries will be likely to lead to higher pensions on retirement. These advantages are compounded by the tax breaks available to pension investments, which, again, disproportionately benefit those who pay taxes, especially at the higher rates. Most private schools (or 'public schools') also benefit from tax support because they can register as charities and so get charitable tax reliefs.

Therefore, while public welfare services largely operate to reduce the disparities of class position, private welfare operates to accentuate these differences and to promote particular advantages for those already enjoying privileged social and economic circumstances. Nevertheless, whatever the advantages and disadvantages of class in access to welfare services, there is the possibility that through social mobility we may be able to alter our class position. This does not apply to some of the other major social divisions that can influence welfare provision.

Gender

Gender is a fundamental social division, separating the population roughly into two halves: men and women. This is a biological division, and it has some important implications for a division of labour based on biological difference. It is women who give birth to children, although once born (and perhaps weaned) it does not need to be women who provide the primary care for them. Gender therefore need not lead to social and economic differences, but, as feminist critics have for some time pointed out, in the UK, and indeed in most societies, it has done, and largely continues to do so.

Feminists have also been critical of some of the organisational features of welfare policy and its outcomes. As mentioned, the post-war welfare state was the high water mark of national collective welfare planning. However, it was introduced by a Labour government comprised almost entirely of men, and it was largely based on a series of assumptions about the respective roles of men and women, which, as feminists later pointed out (Wilson, 1977; Williams, 1989), disadvantaged women. They argued that, as a result of this, welfare was *gendered*, and at the heart of this was what came to be called the 'male breadwinner' model of work and family life.

The male breadwinner model was based on the assumption that in any family the man would be the primary earner and the woman the primary carer, in particular, where there were dependent children. This meant that, among other things, women (especially married women) would not need income protection in employment, as they would not need to work and could rely on support from their husbands. The National Insurance scheme did not, therefore, initially provide protection for married women because, as Beveridge himself argued, they could make 'marriage their sole occupation' (1942, p 49).

In practice, of course, this sharp division of labour did not represent the lives of many families. Even in the immediate post-war years many women (both married and unmarried) worked in the labour market, and in more recent years the numbers in employment have steadily grown, with the employment rate for women now around two thirds, compared to around three quarters for men. What is more, family structures vary and they are changing – not all families fit into the husband and wife with dependent children model.

Formal discrimination against women in social security protection was removed in the 1970s and discrimination on the basis of sex or gender more generally was made unlawful. Nevertheless, the male breadwinner model has continued to lead to disadvantage for women in the labour market. In the 1970s women's average wages were only about 55 per cent of men's, and although this had risen to about 85 per cent by the 2000s (Platt, 2011), it still means that on average women at work earn less.

The other side of the male breadwinner model is the assumption that women will be more likely to, and better able to, undertake (unpaid) caring work at home, in particular, looking after dependent children or vulnerable adults. In the 1980s Finch and Groves (1983) argued that caring often operated as an unrecognised burden on women – *A labour of love*, as they called their book – because of the expectation that women would be natural carers *for* those they cared *about*. In a sense, this is clearly wrong. Men can, and do, care. But the expectations that surround women's role as carers continue to mean that many of the burdens of informal welfare provision fall disproportionately on their shoulders; this is linked to their continuing disadvantage in the labour market too. Even welfare provision specifically targeted to support women as workers and carers, such as maternity leave entitlements, can lead to longer-term disadvantage, as the break in career development that this results in can make it more difficult for women to compete with men for some 'top jobs'.

It is now widely accepted in academic debate and policy development that the gender differences in welfare that disadvantage women should be challenged and removed. In this sense, what is sometimes called 'second wave feminism' has been successful in transforming welfare politics and promoting women's *social* rights (first wave feminism was the activities of the suffragettes and others in promoting women's *civil* rights in the early twentieth century). However, winning the argument in principle has not led in practice to equal treatment throughout society, or across all dimensions of welfare provision. It thus remains important to continue to identify the extent to which welfare is 'gendered' and provide welfare services that help women and men to share their benefits and their responsibilities, rather than reinforcing stereotypes of female and male roles.

Race and ethnicity

In her book criticising the failure of much social policy practice and analysis to recognise and respond to major social divisions, Williams (1989) focused in particular on two dimensions of this: gender, and race and ethnicity. Race and ethnicity are important for welfare, and in the UK we live in an increasingly ethnically diverse society. This is primarily the result of a long history of immigration to the country of people who have brought with them, to some extent, the social and cultural practices of their former homelands. For some, even several generations after initial immigration, these cultural differences have sometimes endured and have enriched the social and cultural environment that we all enjoy. We have all (or most of us) been to 'Indian' or 'Chinese' restaurants – although actually these generic terms cover a wide range of different cuisines and geographical roots, including now those developed in the UK, like Birmingham's *baltis*.

Ethnic diversity is welcomed by many people, although concerns about continuing (allegedly high) levels of immigration to the UK are now often identified as one of the most important political issues in election campaigns. Such opposition to immigration attracts the support of significant minorities in a number of advanced welfare regimes, especially in Europe. What is more, some aspects of ethnic diversity can lead to members of minority ethnic communities being identified, and discriminated against, on the basis of their ethnicity. In particular, this can be the case when skin colour is used to identify ethnic minority groups and to suggest that they are not really British, and therefore should not have the same rights and protections as 'proper' British citizens. This is *racism*. Since the 1970s legislation in the UK has made it unlawful and a range of public agencies have been established to combat it – most recently the Equality and Human Rights Commission.

Despite this official recognition, racism nevertheless remains a potent force in British society, and discrimination against a range of ethnic minority communities and individuals continues to take place, both directly and indirectly – highlighted not so long ago by the police reaction to the murder of the black teenager Stephen Lawrence in London in 1993, which led to a wide-ranging (though not entirely effective) review of the racist and discriminatory practices within the Metropolitan Police Force. Racism can take a number of different forms, and the contributors to Craig et al (2012) provide a good introduction to the importance of these different dimensions of race and ethnicity in the study of social policy. In the context of collective welfare policy, however, the most important underlying feature is the assumption that people from minority ethnic communities may not be entitled to welfare protection because they have not contributed to it.

This is based, in part, on the assumption that immigrants to the UK will not have paid the taxes and NI contributions that fund welfare services. Obviously this does not apply in the case of second and third generation minority ethnic citizens who have lived in the UK all their lives. In any case, however, it is a false assumption, as in practice current welfare services are funded out of current taxation and contributions, so all taxpayers, whenever they arrived in the country, are paying these. There is no logical justification for the argument that any citizens, whatever their ethnicity or immigrant status, have not contributed to the welfare services that they may need to use. However, this exclusionary discourse is sometimes still directed at some ethnic groups, and more recently has been directed in particular towards refugees and asylum seekers, and other recent immigrants to the country.

Racism can, and should, be challenged by ensuring that all citizens, whatever their ethnicity or background, have equal access to their social rights to welfare. Equal expectations and equal treatment need not imply conformity of provision, however. Ethnic and cultural differences sometimes lead to demands for specific forms of welfare services. For example, Muslims may want halal meat to be provided in school dinners for their children and particular dress codes for girls to be permitted within school uniform regulations. Whether such diversity in provision can be accommodated through providing choice for users with different cultural preferences is to a large extent a practical issue, driven by the cost and feasibility of delivering such diversity in services. But there is no reason in principle why such preferences should not be included in the 'voice' of users in debates over service development and delivery. Where these can be met without compromising the standards and accessibility of services for others (as is often the case in the provision of halal meat in school dinners for instance), then ethnic and cultural diversity can be an important dimension of service planning – and of citizen and community engagement in shaping collective welfare.

Disability

It is probably inaccurate to describe ability and disability as a social division, or people with disabilities as a social group. In part, this is because the nature and scale of disability varies so dramatically – from the need for glasses to correct poor eyesight to the partial paralysis that confines someone to a wheelchair, and it includes mental disability, like learning difficulties, as well as physical disability. What is more, disability need not be a barrier to social interaction and engagement. Those of us with glasses usually manage all social interaction as well as those without (including competitive sport), and the Cambridge physicist Stephen Hawking demonstrated so amply that, even when disabled by motor neurone disease and confined to a wheelchair with an electronic voice box, he could become a world leading academic.

Nevertheless, disabilities can inhibit people's ability to participate in some social interaction (Stephen Hawking cannot play physical sports) and, more pertinently, can lead to needs for particular welfare services. The need for specific services for people with different disabilities has been recognised since the early development of welfare services, by private providers (such as opticians) and voluntary organisations (such as the Royal National Institute of Blind People, RNIB), as well as in public services.

There are a range of services in the UK to provide support for people with disabilities, including physical aids (like glasses and wheelchairs), adaptions to homes (like chair lifts), personal care (for help with dressing, washing, shopping or cooking) and, where needs are more extensive, residential care. There are also social security benefits to supplement the incomes of those with particular needs, for instance, what used to be called mobility and attendance benefits (to contribute to the costs of getting out and about or purchasing personal care) and are now covered by the more generic personal independence payment (PIP).

Where this becomes a question of social division and access to collective welfare, is when these services and benefits do not meet the needs of some people with disabilities to participate fully in society. And, given the lower average participation of people with disabilities in the labour market, with less than a half in employment compared to around three quarters of non-disabled people (DWP, 2012), there is some evidence that this is the case. More significantly, in the last few decades in particular, people with disabilities have begun to recognise their common cause as a social group and to campaign for improved service provision. This has included the establishment of campaigning organisations like Disability Rights UK, and the academic and policy analysis of the demands of people with disabilities to be supported to participate fully in an able-bodied world (Oliver, 2009; Shah and Priestley, 2011). It has led too to the introduction of legislation to seek to prevent discrimination against people on account of their disability and to require the inclusion of people in employment.

As disability campaigners point out, with appropriate support people with a range of different disabilities can lead full and active social lives – there have been MPs and members of the House of Lords taking part in the government of the country who are blind, or deaf or using wheelchairs. However, for some of these 'success stories', it has been the individuals' ability to access and purchase private welfare services which has contributed directly or indirectly to their enhanced social participation. Where people with disabilities are disadvantaged as a social group, therefore, it is because our collective welfare services have failed to provide them with the public support and benefits that they need to participate in society. The criticisms voiced by some of the more vocal campaigners for disability rights are a reminder that some of these collective challenges still remain.

Diversity and collectivity

Social divisions create a challenge to the collective provision of welfare. If we are all members of different, disparate and perhaps even conflicting social groups, then to what extent does it make sense to argue that we are all in it together? And how, therefore, can we expect to build collective support for shared investment and redistribution? There are some who argue that because of these social differences we do not really have any shared experiences or interests. This is sometimes referred to by sociologists as a *relativist* argument, and it is often linked to an *interpretivist* approach to analysing social relations. Everyone's experience and knowledge of society is unique it is argued here (and of course at one level this is true); therefore there can be no objective social facts beyond our individual perceptions. Extreme interpretivists reject the *positivists'* view that social relations can be objectively identified and studied.

Where this approach links to relativism in welfare policy is in the (political) argument that no one's perceptions or experiences should be privileged over anyone else's. All experiences are valid, it is alleged; and following this all needs and preferences are legitimate – or at least as legitimate as any others. Relativists recognise, and celebrate, social difference and diversity, and thus are supportive of the claims of different social groups to have different, and even conflicting, demands for recognition and for welfare support. This could mean that members of one cultural group cannot pass judgement on the preferences of others, or that meeting the needs of some groups will inevitably bring these into conflict with the provision that may be being enjoyed by others.

There are problems with this relativism, however, especially in such extreme forms. If all of our experiences and needs are different and distinct, and, if social groups are in practice competing for social support, then how can we develop any collective response to these – and persuade citizens that it is in their collective interests to support this? We can only answer these questions by challenging the premise on which they are made: that is, the interpretivist and relativist argument that social relations are based only on individual perception, and that all social groups are essentially competing for their own interests. This is not a premise that I, and many others, share.

Our individual perceptions do matter, and, as I have explained in this chapter, different social groups do have (some) different experiences and needs. However, as a positivist, I recognise that social relations are also independent of our individual perceptions. Other lives go on when I am asleep, and will continue when I am dead. Yet what happens in these other lives matters to me, both directly and indirectly, and I can study this and respond to it. Indeed, we all have the power, and the responsibility, to understand our social world and to act within it. Although there are differences in the experiences and needs of different social groups, in reality membership of these groups overlaps, and there is much that we all share despite our differences.

Gender, class and ethnicity divide us, but we are all part of more than one of these, and other, social groups – what is referred to now as *intersectionality*. This can create challenges for us when the interests of these groups clash – should Muslim women oppose the separation of boys and girls for some activities in some schools even when religious leaders argue that this is culturally required? But it also alerts us to the fact that we have shared interests across these different groups, for instance, in securing a good school education for all our children.

It is certainly the case that some social groups have been disadvantaged in their access to public welfare: women under the male breadwinner model, or members of minority ethnic communities recently moving to the country in accessing public housing because of the need to meet long-term residence requirement, for example. But these do not undermine the more general value of the provision of these public services. Within them, these exclusionary practices can be challenged and changed, as has largely been the case with residence requirements for public housing.

Indeed, it is in part through the greater recognition of, and challenge to, inappropriate and unjustified exclusion from public services that improvements in these can be achieved that should improve their accessibility – and hence their popularity. At the same time, providing a voice for those from different social groups and minority communities to argue for recognition and flexibility within the planning and delivery of services can also mean that support for public services does not mean support for uniformity of practice or conformity to the models of need and provision determined by others. Our collective response to the diversity of social groups in society can, and should, be one of inclusion to ensure that all can access welfare whatever their circumstances or experiences, and flexibility to meet particular needs where appropriate within broader shared provision. These are processes that have become an important part of policy planning and development, but within which there is still significant progress to be made.

Summary

Like all societies, modern UK society is comprised of different social groups, whose interests may at times diverge and even conflict. These include differences of age, class, gender, ethnicity and ability. We need to recognise the impact of these differences on the development and delivery of welfare services, and where appropriate we need to ensure that these services can respond to the different needs and preferences of different social groups. However, this does not mean that all shared interests and experiences should be abandoned to embrace a relativist position on welfare planning. There is much that we share, despite our differences, and collective welfare policy must recognise the need to balance responsiveness to difference with shared investment for all.

Key texts

The contributors to Payne (2013) provide a good introductory guide to most of the major social divisions in modern UK society. Roberts (2011) is a good introduction to understanding the analysis of class. Although rather dated, Williams (1989) remains an important discussion of why the analysis of gender and ethnicity should be central to our understanding of how social policy operates. Pascall (2012) and Craig et al (2012) contain more recent material on gender and ethnicity in welfare respectively. Oliver (2009) is an engaging discussion of the different dimensions of disability and the policy consequences of this.

7

What challenges does welfare face?

In the early decades of the twenty-first century the collective provision of public welfare faces a number of challenges. These include the conceptual and organisational challenges that I have been discussing in the earlier chapters of this book, but these are largely *endogenous*, or internal, challenges to do with the goals of social policy and its ability to achieve these. In addition to these there are also significant *exogenous*, or external, challenges – changes in the broader social and economic context within which welfare operates, and to which it needs to respond. It is these exogenous challenges that I want to explore in this chapter, to examine to what extent they may threaten, or shape, the future prospects for collective welfare provision. Some more apocalyptic commentators have sometimes talked about these creating a *crisis* for the welfare state or even, in Taylor-Gooby's (2013) analysis, a 'double crisis'. Alternatively, as Pierson (1998) suggested back in the 1990s, they may mean that at the start of the new century we are moving 'beyond the welfare state'.

The time frame through which we might trace back these challenges is to some extent a contested one. As I shall return to discuss in more detail below, some argue that they can be traced back to the economic recession of the 1970s and the collapse of Keynesian economic support for state intervention in the economy, while others point to the wider recessions of the 1980s and the growing impact of greater global economic competition on national public spending plans and commitments. In the UK this was articulated and implemented by a Conservative government under Margaret Thatcher, which was openly critical of the central role of state welfare, and supportive instead of moves towards privatisation and marketisation. Although, as Pierson (1998) and others have argued, this concern about the compatibility of growing state welfare and market competitiveness was felt in most advanced welfare regimes from the 1980s on, and led to moves towards a more widespread 'retrenchment' in national welfare planning.

These challenges have generally been referred to as the product of a move towards a new, neoliberal, approach within political discourse and economic planning, based on the promotion of free market competition and the reduction of public spending commitments. At the beginning of the twenty-first century it is this neoliberal challenge that poses arguably the greatest threat to the future development of public welfare in the UK and beyond, although, as Taylor-Gooby (2013) argued, it is only one dimension of a 'double crisis', for there are other broader social and economic changes underway, which also have an impact on the future development of welfare policy.

Demographic and social trends

Demography is the study of changes in the structure of society caused by population growth and decline, and in particular the analysis of statistical data on the changing balance between different age groups within the population. In this sense, it is a critically important tool for welfare policy planning, for it allows us to predict to a large extent how the structure of the population will change in the future. Most obviously, for example, we know what the future demand for school places will be when today's under-fives reach compulsory school age. When, therefore, we look at the potential changes in the balance between different age groups within the population, we can use demographic projections to estimate how these will develop in the future.

The most important demographic challenge to the future development of welfare for the foreseeable future is the growth in the numbers of older people in the population (as mentioned in Chapter 6). The proportion of the population aged 60–74 is expected to rise from around 14.6 per cent to 16.5 per cent between 2010 and 2030, and the proportion of over 75s even more, from 7.9 per cent to 11.3 per cent (ONS, 2010). This is a rise from around 10 million to over 15 million over 65s, and from 3 million to 6 million over 80s – with these numbers rising further to 19 million and 8 million by 2050. This is part of a broader change in the balance of the population of the UK over the century after 1970, as calculated by the Office for National Statistics, which can be seen in Figure 7.1, which also shows the median age rising from 33 to 44.

Figure 7.1 Percentage age distribution, UK, year ending mid-1971 to year ending mid-2087

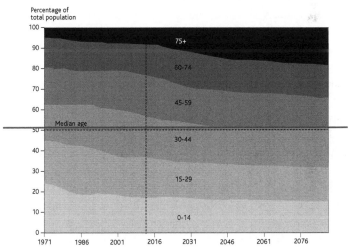

Source: ONS, 2013, Figure 2.3.

At the same time, in many countries, especially those with established welfare states, fertility levels have been declining. For instance, in Germany, Italy and Spain the fertility rate (the average number of births for each woman in the population) is below 1.4, much less than the two births that would at least be needed to maintain current population levels. And the smaller numbers of children being born here will contribute over time to a lower proportion of younger adults within the population as a whole. In the UK (and in the US) fertility rates are currently higher, at just under two, closer to full replacement, and here the changing balance of the population is less dramatic – although, as the figures for the UK above reveal, it is still significant. The consequence of this is that the ratio of households over pension age compared to those of working age is projected to rise from 1:3.2 in 2008 to 1:2.4 in 2035 (ONS, 2010). In simple terms, there will be proportionately fewer adults of working age to support the growing numbers of older people.

In fact, the population of the UK has been growing overall over the last century or so, despite the reductions in fertility. This is mainly due to immigration, with significant numbers of people moving to the country from abroad. As most immigrants are of working age, this has helped to reduce to some extent the shifting balance towards the older generations – though not to reverse it. And in time these former immigrants will add further to the growth in the elderly population as they too reach old age.

The demographic changes taking place in the UK are not, in principle, a new problem. We have always experienced changes in the scale and structure of our population, and, with improved information technology and access to more quantitative data, we can now analyse and predict demographic changes and their potential consequences much more accurately. This means that we can, and indeed must, plan collectively for the future structure of our population and its consequent welfare needs. It is a challenging task, but it is increasingly a well-known and predictable one.

As well as demographic changes, there are also social and economic changes underway that provide new challenges for the future planning of welfare provision. As discussed in Chapter 6, much of the planning for the post-war welfare state was based on a 'male breadwinner' model of labour market participation and family life. This was never the reality for many people and families, but it has become even less so at the beginning of the new century. Female participation in paid employment is almost as extensive as male employment and most women now expect to work, and to combine this with family responsibilities. Family structures also vary significantly from the working husband and dependent wife model, with two-worker and no-worker households, significant numbers of lone parents, and a growing proportion of single person households, especially at the younger and older ranges of the population.

Welfare services need to be flexible enough to respond to the different patterns of employment and family life that people experience, and to some extent this is already the case. Child Tax Credits help to raise the incomes of families of low paid workers, and Child Care Tax Credits can also help to contribute to the costs of expenditure on private child care support for young children in working households. Maternity leave enables women to take time off work for childbirth without having to leave the labour market, and this has now been extended to provide much more limited rights to paternity leave too. More generally, employers are encouraged to consider flexibilities which might make work more 'family friendly', including part-time employment and other forms of flexible working. However, many of these employment-based responses to supporting families are not mandatory, and, as mentioned in Chapter 6, they can also be to some extent counterproductive for women, who may lose out in career progression as a result of periods of maternity leave or part-time working.

As with demographic change, social and economic changes are not new, nor are they unwelcome, and there is no doubt that changes to employment rights and family support have provided real benefits and contributed to greater gender equality, especially in employment. The point is that collective planning for welfare needs continually to identify and respond to such changes. We cannot assume that yesterday's policy assumptions and priorities will be appropriate for tomorrow's social relations; we need to be prepared to adapt to what some sociologists like Giddens (1990) and Beck (1992) have referred to as the new *risks* of modern society, as employment patterns, family lives and cultural preferences change.

In addition to the new risks and pressures of changing social and economic trends, are the greater demands of the users of welfare services that Taylor-Gooby (2013) identified as part of the second dimension of his 'double crisis' of welfare. He argued that, especially in popular services like health and education, new technologies, greater awareness of potential opportunities and support, and shifting cultural expectations were all creating greater pressure on welfare services. In health, improved medical practices (such as keyhole surgery) have increased the availability of and demand for a range of high cost treatments from hip replacements to heart transplants, and new drugs to treat, or alleviate, conditions like AIDS or cancer are increasingly available, but are often also very expensive. In education, ever larger proportions of young (and older) people want to go to university, and smaller class sizes in schools are generally linked to improved learning and achievement for pupils.

These increased expectations of welfare provision are common across all welfare regimes, and in one sense, of course, are a positive reminder of the value that people place on these services. We increasingly expect our modern societies to be able to respond to our more extensive and more sophisticated welfare needs. And in this sense they are also a basis for continuing popular support for collective responses to these. However, they inevitably create challenges for the future development of public services to meet these demands, especially when, at the same time, there is evidence that public attitudes towards investment in public welfare are not so supportive.

Public attitudes and media discourses

Critical to any argument making the case for collective investment in welfare services are public attitudes towards welfare spending and investment, in particular, the perceptions people hold of the value of benefits and services, and their support (or not) for increased investment in these. Of course, we do not really know what people think about these things, but we can get a good idea from the answers that those questioned give in surveys asking them about their attitudes to various key welfare issues. Here the evidence base in the UK is quite good, because for over three decades annual national surveys of public attitudes have been conducted, exploring much the same basic issues. Currently carried out by NatCen Social Research, these are called the British Social Attitude Surveys (BSA), and the most recent (BSA32, based on the 2014 survey) contains a chapter on 'Benefits and welfare', written by Taylor-Gooby and Taylor (2015).

The evidence on attitudes towards investment in welfare from the BSA is not encouraging, and indeed reveals that attitudes towards increased spending, especially on particular groups, has been hardening over the last two decades or so. In general, public welfare does not seem to be as popular as it was in the UK, and in this sense public attitudes may be reflecting the individualistic ideology of neoliberalism, that I discuss in more detail below. However, the picture that emerges from the most recent survey data is rather more complex than a general lack of support for public welfare, with some areas of spending attracting more support than others.

Overall support for an increase in taxation to fund additional spending on health, education and social benefits fell from 63 per cent in 2002 to 32 per cent in 2010, rising slightly to 37 per cent in 2014 – from two thirds down to one third. Within this, however, as reported elsewhere by Taylor-Gooby (2013), support for spending on health (between 40 and 50 per cent) and education (between 25 and 30 per cent) has generally been higher than support for social security benefits (below 5 per cent and declining). And within social security spending there are different priorities too: when asked to select their top two priorities for spending here, 67 per cent chose pensions, 60 per cent disabled people and only 13 per cent the unemployed (Taylor-Gooby and Taylor, 2015). As mentioned before, therefore, it is the universal services of health and education that appear to attract most support, together with the horizontal distribution effect of life course 'savings'.

Behind this mixed, but nevertheless declining, support for public welfare are also hardening attitudes towards the needs of some welfare recipients and the extent to which their social rights are deserving of support. When asked whether benefits levels were too high and so discouraged work, 52 per cent said yes in 2014 – almost double the proportion, 28 per cent, in 1997; conversely, the proportion believing that they were too low and causing hardship fell over the same period from 55 to 27 per cent. Similarly, those believing that most people in their area could get a job if they wanted one rose from 27 per cent in 1993 to 59 per cent in 2014. And over the last three decades between 30 and 40 per cent have consistently said that they believed that most people on the dole were 'fiddling' their entitlement (Taylor-Gooby and Taylor, 2015), although as reported in Chapter 4, actually the recorded level of fraud is less than one per cent.

The BSA is only a survey, but it has a strong and reliable pedigree among statisticians, and so its findings are generally taken seriously by commentators, as Taylor-Gooby (2013) discusses in his book on the 'double crisis' of welfare. They reveal that people overestimate problems like benefit fraud and the so-called 'unemployment trap' that are discussed in Chapter 4. As a consequence of this, they are less sympathetic to arguments for expanding, or even maintaining, support for social security benefits which redistribute on a vertical basis to those out of work. Improved support for those outside the labour market will therefore be difficult to argue for, especially in isolation from other forms of collective support.

Even for the more popular areas of collective welfare like health, education and retirement pensions, however, it seems that support for increased spending on these has been drastically reduced over the last two decades or so. What is more, this support was in decline prior to the economic recession of 2008/09 and the austerity policies introduced since 2010 to reduce the deficit in overall UK public spending, which I discuss below. With the 2015 election revealing continued general support for a government committed to reducing public spending in this way, it could be more and more difficult to turn around these negative attitudes towards improved collective welfare.

Public attitudes may also be influenced by media coverage of welfare issues. The aim of most mainstream media, principally broadcasting and newspapers, is to inform the public. Nevertheless, to some extent those in control in these media are bound to use their products to reflect wider public opinion – in the case of newspapers, in order to sell these to as many people as possible. But, of course, they may also use their power to seek actively to shape opinion. This is certainly the case with some newspapers, such as the *Daily Mail* and *The Sun*, which have sometimes used a campaigning style to denounce welfare 'scroungers' or 'immigrants' as undeserving of public support, and which, along with most other papers, actively seek to influence public opinion at the time of democratic elections.

In 1982 Golding and Middleton published a path-breaking study of media coverage of welfare issues called *Images of welfare*, which revealed a general hostility towards benefit claimants in particular across much of the popular press. And more recent commentators such as Toynbee and Walker (2015) and O'Hara (2014), have continued to point to the negative imagery towards some welfare service users still employed by sections of the press. Negative imagery can be found in the broadcast media too, notably in a Channel 4 series aired in 2014 based in a road in Birmingham where relatively high levels of benefit claimants lived. It was called *Benefits Street*, and it presented a largely unsympathetic portrayal of local residents as undeserving of public support.

The majority of newspapers in the UK are owned by proprietors openly on the right of the political spectrum, and they adhere largely to a neoliberal ideology of individualism and self-reliance, rather than collective responsibility. Their power and influence may partly explain the increasingly unsympathetic attitudes towards improved collective welfare revealed in the attitude surveys. Although we should be cautious not to overestimate the influence of the popular press, not least because only a (declining) minority of the population buy newspapers.

One of the reasons for the declining reach of these traditional media outlets has been the rapid growth, in particular over the last decade, of online and internet communications – so-called *social media*. With the advent of Google searches, Wikipedia and Facebook connections there are many more sources of information for people to turn to, and now they can do this anywhere and anytime on smartphones carried in their pockets or bags. What is more, information can be shared and promoted through online blogs and campaigns, and even more ubiquitously through Twitter. For many, especially in younger generations, these social media have replaced traditional media as the first, or only, sources of information and exchange. Here attitudes are inevitably more diverse, and also can be changed much more quickly.

Popular attitudes towards welfare are therefore likely to be shaped by a wider range of outlets and discourses in the future. This may be likely to make it harder for a neoliberal hegemony to be sustained, as had been the case in the popular press in the UK over previous decades. It can also provide a range of fora for the promotion of alternative discourses, which in the past may have had little traction in much popular debate – although changes in the means of communication are no guarantee that changes in the message will necessarily follow. As I shall return to discuss in Chapter 8, this will require coordinated leadership to promote different messages through a range of different outlets, both formal and informal.

Technological progress and environmental sustainability

Since the creation of the welfare state in the middle of the last century, the pace of technological change has continued to grow ever more rapidly. Those who have lived through these decades will have seen more such change in their lifetimes than would have occurred over several centuries in the past; and there is little doubt that the scale and pace of change will continue to accelerate, at least in the foreseeable future.

Changes in manufacturing and communication technology have transformed the work that we do. Manufacturing can increasingly be done by robots, and communication technology means that markets and products are organised globally. These changes have altered labour markets and the role of employment in supporting people and families. Few jobs are now secure for life – as many would have been just half a century ago. More people are working 'flexibly', perhaps on part-time or temporary contracts – even so-called 'zero hours' contracts which change from day to day. Education and training is also no longer a simple or 'one-off' process, with people now expecting to have to train and retrain more than once over the course of their working lives and to access education provision on a 'lifelong learning' basis at different ages for different purposes.

These labour market changes are another dimension of the new 'risks' identified by authors like Giddens (1990) and Beck (1992). They have led to a more fractured workforce, who may no longer share similar needs for many welfare services, like further and higher education. Although the uncertainty that these new risks entail is itself in another sense a common experience leading to common interests in ensuring that new risks can be identified and met. Our working lives may be more fragmented, but arguably we retain a common interest in collective support to help us respond to this.

As mentioned above, other dimensions of technological change are creating different pressures on welfare services. These include the advances in medical technology and drug treatments, and the more general advances in health and social care services. They mean that people are living longer, but in some cases with significant disabilities, and that the treatments and services that support them are becoming more extensive – and more expensive. This is to be welcomed, but it will also require increased commitments to maintain its progress, and its influence, especially if the benefits of these new advances are to be available to all who could benefit from them, and not just the few who can afford expensive private provision.

As every history of public welfare provision reveals, of course, in the past welfare provision has adapted and grown in the face of challenges posed by new technologies and their economic and social consequences. In large part this has been possible because these changes have also led to continued expansion of economic performance and a growing national and international wealth to underwrite increased public expenditure. Economic growth has meant that improved services can be paid for from the fruits of expanding production.

However, there are increasing numbers of commentators who are concerned about the longer term sustainability of our current models of economic growth. This is because they remain heavily dependent upon the consumption of fossil fuels, which scientists have demonstrated is leading to long-term climate change across the globe. Climate change and environmental sustainability are creating new challenges for social policy planning, which to some extent are in conflict with the models of economic growth that have so far underpinned the expansion of previous welfare provision.

The challenges of environmental sustainability include the insecurity imposed by more extreme climatic events such as floods and droughts. These are felt across the world, but are likely to become more common in the UK too. To combat this and promote more sustainable economic development, we need to reduce fossil fuel consumption, for instance, through the use of carbon taxes. However, these may limit economic growth and impact more severely on those (people and countries) least able to afford them. Alternative sources of energy require significant investment and may, in the short to medium term at least, lead to higher prices for energy, again affecting the poorest most. There has been some international agreement about the need to respond to climate change, most notably the Kyoto Protocol in the 1990s, which purportedly committed developed countries to cutting their emissions by an average of around five per cent by 2012. But many, including the US, did not meet these targets, and international agreement has proved hard to secure. The more recent United Nations climate change conference in Paris in 2015 led to a significant international agreement to cut emissions over the coming decades, although it remains to be seen whether all will be able to implement these.

Collective investment in a range of measures to promote more sustainable living could nevertheless be promoted nationally, and could help to avoid some of the more regressive effects of just increasing costs to discourage carbon emissions. For instance, grants for the refitting of houses to encourage energy efficiency or installation of solar panels, investment in more sustainable transport systems to discourage road use, or strategic use of urban ('brownfield') land for expansion of housing provision.

Going further than this, politicians and commentators who promote a 'greener' agenda for policy development have argued that we may need to accept that past levels of economic growth are not going to be sustainable in the longer term, and that social and economic policy planning must adjust to a low-growth or no-growth future, in which existing resources are shared more equally and a more localised, community-led, form of economic development is promoted. This is close to some of the policies promoted by politicians in the Green Party in the UK, and elsewhere. However, they are very much on the margins of practical political and policy change; it remains the case that, in the short term at least, economic growth will continue to be a necessary complement to investment in the provision of welfare.

Economic pressures

The early part of the twentieth century saw the beginnings of public welfare provision in the UK. This resulted in an initial growth in the spending on health, education and social security as a proportion of gross domestic product (GDP). However, this growth in welfare was contingent to some extent on the broader performance of the economy and the political reaction to this, and when the major economic recession of the 1930s began, this relative growth in welfare spending turned into a decline, as social security spending in particular was cut back. This set something of a pattern for the further development of welfare spending, and its relationship with economic growth and recession. Following the establishment of the welfare state after the Second World War, spending began to grow once more, but declined again after that initial spurt, once the Conservative Party came back into power in the 1950s.

As Figure 7.2 reveals, since the 1940s, welfare spending as a proportion of GDP has risen and declined on a number of occasions, reaching its highest point in the mid-1970s under the then Labour government and declining fitfully after that until the Labour governments of the 2000s raised it once again. Since the recession of 2008 and the public spending reductions of the Coalition and the Conservatives it has fallen again, and according to official projections is set to decline further to below the level of the 1940s. Clearly, therefore, the relative commitment to public

Figure 7.2 Social spending as a percentage of GDP

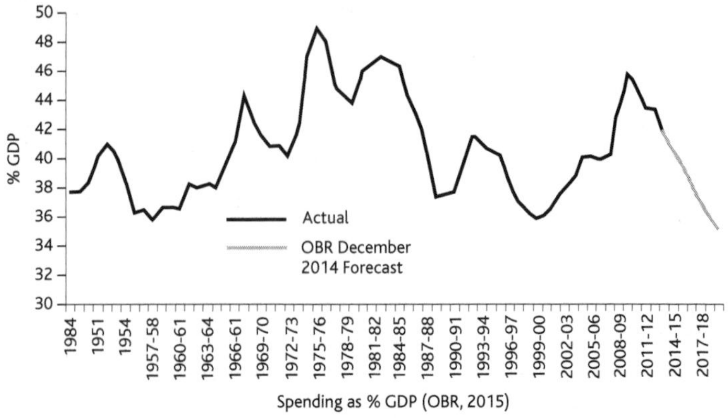

Spending as % GDP (OBR, 2015)

Source: Adapted from OBR, 2015 (Chart 4.9, p 170)

spending over time in the UK has been far from consistent. It has been affected by economic and political changes, and despite some of the growing demands outlined above, its future projections suggest a return to the levels below the early years of the welfare state.

The economic and political contingency of social spending is true for all welfare regimes, as Hay and Wincott (2012) discuss in the case of Europe. However, the patterns of UK spending are a product of the particular circumstances of the country, and especially since the 1970s have seen significantly harsher reductions in proportionate commitments to welfare at times of economic decline.

The rise in spending to the post-war high point in the 1970s was brought to an end by the global economic recession precipitated by the massive rise in the price of oil introduced by the major oil producing countries in 1973. The UK was hit particularly hard by this recession and had to turn to the International Monetary Fund (IMF) for financial support, in return for which the country was required to cut back on its plans for public spending. The Labour Prime Minister of the time, Jim Callaghan, was famously quoted as saying that this revealed that the country could no longer "spend its way out of a recession". This was based on a wider fear that rising public spending would 'crowd out' private investment in market-led economic growth, articulated at the time by the right wing critics Bacon and Eltis (1976).

In the 1980s Labour was replaced by a Conservative government, led by Margaret Thatcher, which was more openly committed to the Bacon and Eltis line that public expenditure and indeed state intervention more generally were damaging market competition. As Figure 7.2 reveals, this government presided over a major decline in public spending back to early post-war levels. As with the growth of welfare in the previous decades, this retrenchment in social spending was experienced in most advanced welfare regimes in the 1980s, but, as, for example, Pierson (1998) argued, the scale and structure of this varied, with the UK taking a tougher political and economic line on the need to cut public welfare.

A return to economic growth in the 2000s, and a return to Labour governments, under Tony Blair, resulted in a return to increased spending as a proportion of GDP, with rises in spending being particularly significant in health and education. Overall, this took the UK back to around the average levels of spending recorded by OECD countries. However, in 2008 there was another major economic recession, the worst since the 1930s, triggered by the collapse of international confidence in bank lending (see Alcock with May, 2014, Ch 15), and in the 2010 UK general election Labour were replaced by a Conservative-led Coalition government.

The recession of the late 2000s was an international phenomenon, particularly affecting most OECD countries. The response of many, including initially the UK, was to maintain public spending to counter the deflationary impact of recession, but this led to much increased levels of public borrowing in most countries. This was a particular problem in some EU countries, such as Greece, Spain and Ireland, which were also members of the common currency Eurozone. This meant that they could be supported by 'bail-out' packages from the European Central Bank, but had to make major cutbacks in public spending, which threw some of them, notably Greece, into a further spiral of economic decline.

The UK was not a member of the Eurozone, but the Coalition government elected in 2010 also undertook a review of public spending commitments and committed the country to a programme of major reductions in this, with the aim of reducing, and then removing, the high levels of public borrowing and eventually eliminating the accumulated public sector deficit. Within this, spending on the NHS and some aspects of education were protected from the highest levels of cuts, with the burden therefore falling more heavily on other areas, notably local authority spending. However, the impact of recession, including the continuing problems in the Eurozone, where the UK's main trading partners lay, made the achievement of the reduced borrowing targets impractical; as a result, the programme of public spending cuts had to be continued by the Conservative government elected in 2015.

These spending cuts have been referred to by commentators as heralding a period of *public austerity* in the country. As the projections in Figure 7.2 reveal, they will be likely to take public spending as a proportion of GDP back down below the levels experienced before the implementation of the post-war welfare state. And, as Taylor-Gooby (2013, p 4) points out, this will also take the UK below the levels of all of the major (G7) economies, including the US, which has traditionally had lower levels of public welfare spending but higher levels of private welfare provision.

Despite the potentially harsh consequences of this public austerity, the assumption that the only practical way to respond to the pressures created by economic recession is to cut back on public expenditure, in particular, on welfare, has become a widespread political and economic assumption over recent decades. Since Callaghan's response to the IMF in the 1970s, most governments (and most economists) have accepted that 'you cannot spend your way out of a recession', and so, as Figure 7.2 reveals, spending levels have been reduced on a number of occasions following economic downturns.

What is more, it seems that the deeper the recession, the harsher the cutbacks in expenditure. This has certainly been the case with the austerity measures introduced since 2010, despite the commitments to seek to protect some spending on health and education. Indeed, in part because of this, the cutbacks elsewhere have been even harsher, with social security support for those of working age taking the largest reductions. The election in 2015 of the Conservative government, under David Cameron, who had led the Coalition, seemed to be evidence that a majority of the electorate also supported, or accepted, the case for public spending cuts to reduce public sector deficits. Further reductions are planned by the new government through to 2020, including around £12 billion in cuts to social security spending. These involve not only reductions in the tax credits for workers on low pay, but also significant cuts in support for families and younger adults, while pensions and other benefits for older claimants were largely protected – something of a shift in the horizontal impact of welfare retrenchment away from the growing numbers of older beneficiaries.

Public austerity is not without its costs. Reductions in public spending are bound to affect the lives of many. These include the public sector service workers who have lost their jobs, with local authority employment in particular being dramatically scaled back in many areas. However, it is those using, and depending on, welfare services who inevitably are hardest hit. And, with most of the cuts falling on social security benefits for working age families and young adults, it is these groups who have had to adjust the most, and, if current trends continue, will continue to need to do so in the near future.

Some of the broader implications of the Coalition's austerity policies between 2010 and 2015 were discussed in a trenchant critique of government policy by Toynbee and Walker (2015). A more detailed, and harrowing, exploration of the impact of austerity was provided by O'Hara (2015), who spent 12 months travelling through the country exposing some of the costs of austerity for large numbers of ordinary citizens. O'Hara explored experiences of problems like hunger, debt, worklessness, disability and insecurity. She exposed the increasing reliance of people on food banks (over 300,000 people in 2013) and 'payday lenders' offering short-term loans at astronomical rates of interest to those unable to get credit elsewhere. Box 7.1 captures her experiences of visiting a food bank and a community centre in 2012 and 2013.

Box 7.1 Austerity bites

Inside the church hall the bags go swiftly. Some people enter, pick up supplies and leave right away, embarrassed expressions on their faces ... Two young teenage volunteers helping lay out bags of food on the wooden trestle tables explain that they don't want to be formally interviewed because they are humiliated at needing to fetch food for their mother. They volunteer, they explain, because by doing so they feel that the food has been earned. It is not a hand-out that way, they say … There is no sign whatsoever of people taking food (as ministers repeatedly alleged) not out of need but because it was available. (O'Hara, 2015, pp 17–18).

In the café people sit around drinking coffee and chatting. It looks and feels like a welcoming space – and it is. However, the reason the centre was so busy in the spring of 2013 was because of debt. Over the previous few months the centre had seen its debt advice service swamped by people with acute debt problems and, according to one worker at the centre, … demand was expected to keep on rising as more cuts kicked in. (p 82)

Along with other authors writing about the experiences of poverty and deprivation in the early twenty-first century, like McKenzie (2015), O'Hara provided an insight into the human face of economic austerity – but one which so far has not changed the dominant assumptions behind economic planning. The supposed need to cut back on welfare spending in response to economic recession has become established as the practical basis for economic planning in the UK, and elsewhere, at the beginning of the new century, but it is also part of a wider political discourse, which ultimately can be contested and challenged.

Political discourse and policy debate

Political discourses are informed by, or situated within, political ideologies. Academics writing about political ideologies generally group these into a broad typology, moving from left to right across the political spectrum: from socialism to social democracy to conservatism to neoliberalism. These were explained in the context of social policy by George and Wilding in 1994, and they have also been summarised more recently by some of the contributors to *The student's companion to social policy* (Alcock et al, 2016). Some critics have argued, however, that this left to right continuum is too narrow to capture the diversity to be found in political ideologies, especially over the last few decades. These include ideologies linked to social movements, like feminism or anti-racism, or those seeking to challenge both left and right approaches, such as 'green' or environmental politics (see Fitzpatrick, 2001). More generally, some have argued that it is particular issues that increasingly drive the political discourses and political preferences of many people, such as community, insecurity, technology or crime (see Fitzpatrick, 2005), leading to what some have called the popularity of 'single issue' politics.

The problem with single issue politics is that it can lead to a fragmentation of political allegiances and political engagement, which makes it much more difficult to encourage people to take an interest in, or become active in, the broader political decision making that inevitably has to take place in democratic societies. This is a problem which is explored in more detail by Stoker (2006) in his book on *Why politics matters*. However, despite the rise in single issue politics, it is the broader political discourses that have been most influential in shaping welfare policy and practice throughout its development over the last century or so.

It was social democracy that was the driving political force behind the development of the welfare state in the middle of the last century. This was true not just in the UK, but in the welfare regimes of most advanced industrial countries (see Pierson, 1998; Castles, 2004). Central to social democracy was a belief that capitalist economies could, and should, be transformed by the introduction of public welfare services to protect citizens from the failure of the free market to meet many of their welfare needs, and that once established, these public services would support the future development of capitalist economic growth, for instance, by ensuring the provision of a healthy and well-educated workforce and by intervening to promote investment in infrastructure like housing and transport. This would also make public welfare politically popular, as all would have an interest in protecting and developing it (Therborn and Roebroek, 1986).

As explained above, however, following the economic recessions of the 1970s and early 1980s, this faith in the desirability and affordability of public welfare was questioned. In particular, it was argued that the demands for improvements in public welfare would continue to drive up public spending. It was thought that as a result investment in private market growth would be 'crowded out', leading to an overall decline in economic performance, which, it was claimed, was what had begun to happen in the last quarter of the last century. This critique of social democracy was generally referred to as neoliberalism, and, like social democracy, it had an international reach.

Classic liberalism was the nineteenth-century idea that economic growth was the product of free market competition without interventions by government to control investment or spending – referred to at the time as *laissez-faire*, or leave alone. Neoliberalism was thus a twentieth-century adaptation of this, in the context of welfare capitalist economies, which had developed extensive state intervention and service provision, and now needed to reverse this as far as possible.

Neoliberals therefore argue for a return to the free market – although it is debatable whether, even in the nineteenth century, capitalist markets were really free from government. More specifically, they argue for a reduced role for the state, and reductions in state expenditure – not just as a response to economic recession, but in order to promote instead a mixed economy of welfare providers and more individual responsibility for meeting, and paying for, welfare needs. In 2010 the UK Coalition government referred to this as the promotion of a 'Big Society', as an alternative to the big state of the post-war welfare settlement; and argued that citizens, communities and voluntary organisations should play a greater role, alongside private companies, in replacing the 'monopolistic' public services of the welfare state.

This individualism within neoliberalism is linked to a different approach to inequality and social justice to that promoted by social democracy, and discussed in Chapter 2. In particular, neoliberals do not see inequality as a social problem, but rather as a potential driver of economic and social development, with those who 'create' wealth being rewarded by high incomes and capital gains, which then indirectly 'trickle down' to the rest of the population as a result of the ensuing economic growth that their spending promotes.

There is no doubt that inequality has grown significantly in the UK, and elsewhere, over the last few decades, as discussed in Chapter 2. Atkinson (2015) has mapped this in more detail, describing it as the 'inequality turn' of neoliberalism – and outlining a series of proposals to promote greater equality. As Sayer (2015) also explains, it is the very rich in particular, the top 1%, who have benefited most from this recent growth in inequality, although there is little evidence that this has trickled down to the rest of society, or been of any benefit to social and economic development more generally. Indeed, arguably it was the ever increasing rewards received by those manipulating the credit driven economic growth of the early twenty-first century that led to the financial collapse of 2007 and 2008, and consequently to the rising public indebtedness which has been the primary justification for further austerity in public services.

Whatever the causes of economic change, however, a neoliberal orthodoxy of individualism and greater inequality, and privatisation and competition in a mixed economy of welfare provision, has come to dominate political discourse in the UK in the 2010s, and to lead to significant changes in policy direction towards the scaling back of the welfare state. In neoliberalism, therefore, there is a political ideology that acts as rationale for the reductions in public welfare provision resulting from economic austerity. Not only can we no longer afford a welfare state, any extensive commitments to public welfare also undermine individual responsibility and stifle the market-driven growth in competition and choice.

This dominance of neoliberal political ideology has been questioned more recently by some European academics, however, who have suggested that both the social democratic and the neoliberal approaches to welfare policy may be being challenged, and even replaced, by a focus instead on welfare as a form of social investment – the move to what is sometimes called a 'social investment state' (Morel et al, 2012).

In the social investment state, the 'passive' welfare support of the old welfare state, based on Marshall's social rights, is replaced by a focus on the 'active' role that welfare services and benefits can play in supporting broader social and economic development. For instance, education is argued to be an investment in human capital, in particular in equipping future generations for employment in an increasingly skills-based labour market; child care is seen as supporting families to remain active in the labour market; and social security support is linked to help for unemployed workers to learn new skills and gain labour market experiences through employment support and activation schemes.

The social investment state also challenges the neoliberal view of welfare spending as a 'drain' on the development of capitalist markets. Through investment in human capital, by encouraging and supporting the unemployed to return to the labour market, and, of course, in maintaining a fit and healthy population, investment in welfare is actually supporting economic growth, not inhibiting it.

The contributors to Morel at al (2012) point out that to some extent the social investment state is an ideologically informed discourse rather than a clear political and policy programme, and that different welfare regimes in Europe demonstrate different levels of engagement with the social investment model. It is stronger in some regimes – such as Scandinavia and northern continental Europe – than others, and stronger in some areas of provision – such as education and employment support – than others. And in the UK in particular, the picture is rather a mixed one. The education and welfare to work policies of the Labour governments under Blair were evidence of some political commitment to an investment approach to welfare spending. However, the cutbacks in public spending, especially longer-term strategic spending on things like schools and hospitals, and the hostility towards support for unemployed workers, suggest that under the Coalition and the Conservatives, neoliberal thinking has remained a dominating force.

It is only to be expected, of course, that political ideologies will compete for dominance, and that within particular regimes, and over time, the balance of influence over policy development will vary. In the UK, as I have argued above, there has been a significant shift towards neoliberal approaches since the economic recessions of the 1970s and 1980s. But elements of support for comprehensive social democratic welfare services still remain, most notably perhaps in public support for the NHS. And in the Labour administrations of the early twentieth century in particular, there is evidence of the promotion of welfare as an investment in the social and economic development of the country, with rights to welfare being linked to responsibilities for citizens to be active in pursuing training opportunities and labour market participation. The future of welfare in the country may therefore rest on our ability to recognise the challenges posed by this shifting ideological balance, and to seek to shift the direction of travel towards support for more collective investment in welfare.

Summary

At the beginning of the twenty-first century welfare states, including the UK, face a series of challenges, which some have even called a 'crisis in welfare'. These challenges come from changes in our social structure and our social relations – the risks that we face and the expectations that we have of welfare provision. They are affected too by public attitudes towards collective investment in welfare, which have been hardening, and media discourses which sometimes demonise public welfare and those who rely on it. As well as these social factors, there are also technological and environmental pressures on welfare states, which potentially threaten the settlement between economic growth and welfare expansion that underpinned much of the development of the post-war welfare state.

Since the 1970s and 1980s economic changes have created ever greater pressure to contain, or to reduce, collective expenditure on public welfare, leading most recently to the major cutbacks introduced by the Conservative-led Coalition government following the recession of 2008. These have resulted in a period of 'public austerity', which is likely to take investment in public services back to the levels found before the expansion of the welfare state. This economic austerity is underpinned by a political discourse of neoliberalism, which promotes market competition and individual choice and responsibility over collective investment in welfare. Neoliberalism is a powerful ideology, but it is not totally dominant. In particular, it has been challenged in the UK and continental Europe by those arguing the case for welfare as a collective social investment in economic and social development. The main challenge that we face in promoting such investment is the need to re-establish popular support for collective, rather than individual, responses to the challenges the welfare faces.

Key texts

Taylor-Gooby's (2013) book on the 'double crisis' of welfare is an excellent exploration of many of the social and economic factors providing the external challenges to welfare policy planning. O'Hara's (2014) study of the impact of austerity is harrowing, but it provides a forceful 'bottom-up' perspective on the consequences of cutbacks in welfare provision. Fitzpatrick (2011) contains a range of contributions on the impact of environmental factors on social policy. Hutton (1995, 2002 and 2013) has published three books providing accessible accounts of the development of the UK economy and its response to the 2008 economic recession. Ellison (2006) and Hay and Wincott (2012) discuss the influence of neoliberalism on the wider development of welfare regimes. Stoker (2006) explains why political debate and political engagement are so important for the effective functioning of democratic societies.

8

A new case for collective welfare

In Chapter 7 I outlined a series of challenges facing the collective provision of welfare in the twenty-first century, in particular the willingness of people to pay for increased investment in welfare – or more accurately perhaps, the willingness of politicians to actively promote such investment. Together, these challenges place increasing demands on welfare provision, and at the same time question our ability to supply these services. This is what Taylor-Gooby (2013) called the 'double crisis' of the welfare state. As he also explained, the response to this crisis faces a 'welfare trilemma': we need to provide generous and inclusive welfare to secure collective support; this must be seen as feasible by politicians and voters; and it must be effective in delivering its intended outcomes and in meeting people's needs.

The dominance of neoliberalism in political discourse and economic planning makes responding to this trilemma more daunting, focusing attention instead on individual freedom of choice and responsibility, and seeking to reduce public spending and state intervention in favour of market competition. Tackling the welfare trilemma, therefore, will require us to provide (and promote) an alternative political discourse to neoliberalism. This chapter outlines what this could be, and how it could provide an answer to the question of why we need welfare.

The welfare state and the welfare society

The creation of the welfare state in the mid twentieth century placed collective provision for welfare needs at the centre of social and economic planning, supported and articulated by Beveridge's

(1942) arguments for social support and Keynes' (1936) arguments for state-led economic development. Despite the criticisms that have since been made of the post-war welfare state, and the partial retreat from the universal services initially envisaged, especially after the 1980s, the survey evidence quoted in Chapter 7 suggests that there is still support for the welfare state (or at least parts of it), and this is also still reflected in political discourse and democratic support:there were pledges to protect, or increase, public spending on health and education from all parties in the 2015 UK election.

The welfare state is not dead. However, it is important to remember that it has also never completely dominated welfare provision in the UK, or indeed elsewhere. Private, voluntary and informal provision has always been there for some welfare needs, and there has been a shifting balance over time between the scale and scope of these different sectors, with private and voluntary welfare increasing in significance in recent decades. These different forms of provision have resulted in the mixed economy of welfare discussed in Chapter 1, and have prompted some commentators to argue that, rather than a welfare state, we have, or should have, a 'welfare society'.

This distinction is similar in some ways to the 'Big Society' discourse promoted by the Coalition government of 2010–15 in the UK, which I also mentioned in Chapter 1. The Prime Minister, David Cameron, presented the Big Society as an alternative to the 'big state', arguing that extensive (and expensive) state provision was stifling the appetite (and scope) for individual and community action and market competition (Cameron, 2009). In fact, the Big Society never took off in the UK in the early 2010s, in part because need for, and support for, state services remained. What is more, the community activity promoted in the Big Society was itself often supported by the state, and was often concerned to encourage, rather than replace, public investment in welfare.

The Big Society and the big state were therefore seen by many not as alternative models for welfare support, but as complementary means of achieving this. This is also the case with the welfare state and the welfare society. A welfare society, one in which it is recognised that meeting welfare needs is a desirable social goal, needs a welfare state. For only in a society where there is public provision for key welfare needs, can all citizens and communities act effectively to achieve other social and individual goals. In Sen's (2009) terms, as discussed in Chapter 2, only then do they have the 'capability' to live the lives that they want. Beveridge argued in 1942 that the existence of ignorance, disease, squalor, idleness and want would prevent us from achieving a welfare society; though the language may have changed, this is still the case today.

The social investment state that I discussed in Chapter 7 goes some way towards making the case for a renewed integration of social and economic planning, based on the notion of welfare as an investment in the (human and social) capital needed for successful economic growth. And it is certainly the case that the securing and maintaining of a healthy, well-educated and trained workforce, with support to encourage those who need it to move from 'welfare to work', are essential elements of successful economies in the twenty-first century. But there is more to the economic and social case for collective welfare than this investment in economic growth.

Public goods

One of the reasons for the introduction of public welfare in the twentieth century was the failure of capitalist markets to provide for the welfare needs of all citizens, as Fabians like Sidney and Beatrice Webb argued at the time (Webb, 1911). Some economists have argued that this 'market failure' creates a climate in which public goods have to be provided collectively. Public goods do not just benefit the individuals who might otherwise be able to buy them in a private market because they are 'non-excludable' (see Glennerster, 2003, pp 20–27). Roads, policing, public health and a range of other collectively provided goods cannot be exclusively purchased by individuals, because others will also benefit from them. Therefore the way to ensure that they are provided for those who need them (arguably all of us) is through non-market collective action – as the American economist and philosopher Michael Sandel (2012) has argued, there are limits to the role that markets can play in meeting public needs.

Market failure does not only include the need for the provision of public goods; it also applies to their accessibility and use. This is because the potential consumers of public goods (and services) will often not have the knowledge or ability to choose them, as they might in an open market. This is most obviously the case in healthcare, where we are unlikely to know (or even understand) our medical condition or what might be done to cure or relieve it. But it also applies in areas like education (what is the best school for our children?) and long-term social care (when might we need to access personal care support?).

As well as this information weakness for consumers there are also information problems for would-be market suppliers, which in effect mean that markets will be likely to fail to meet many welfare needs. This is particularly the case for the availability of private insurance, which might be seen as a means of funding the private purchase of welfare services for many who cannot afford upfront costs, because in practice the markets for private insurance are also not viable for all. Providers of health insurance may not know about the health conditions of their potential clients, which may make them reluctant to provide cover for some health needs (such as AIDS) or to some client groups (such as diabetics). Private insurance companies will inevitably want to avoid 'bad risks', and so will be unlikely to provide (affordable) cover for all cases – referred to by economists as *cream-skimming*. Thus private insurance is not an effective protection for all needs and for all citizens, with those in the greatest need and with the least resources most likely to be excluded from it. This is just what has happened in the private healthcare insurance market in the US, where many of those at the bottom of the income distribution were not able to afford adequate health insurance and so have had to rely on the public safety net provision, *Medicaid*.

We need public provision for collective welfare because private markets will fail to provide it, or in some cases to provide it in accessible forms and at affordable prices for all. What is more, this need for collective welfare investment in public goods has a (much more important) longer-term dimension. Public investments in roads, schools and hospitals do not just benefit current users; these investments will be there for future generations too. This is true of investment in the training of teachers and doctors, who will be able to teach and treat our children, and even in researchers who are seeking to discover new cures for diseases or better ways of providing services. This wider benefit from economic investment in public goods has been called the 'common good', and I shall return to its important role in the case for welfare shortly.

There is a further development of the argument for investment in public goods, however, which has both economic and ideological dimensions. As I mentioned in Chapter 2, Wilkinson and Pickett (2009) produced evidence that greater inequality within societies was associated with higher levels of health and social problems. There are no doubt a number of reasons for this connection, but there are two consequences of more extreme inequality which are likely to be particularly important to support for and access to welfare.

- At the top end of our unequal society some people will be able (and willing) to buy private goods and services where they can, for instance, private school (or 'public school') places for their children or preferential health treatment outside the NHS. As economists point out, these private services are frequently 'free-riding' on the collective investment in the training of teachers and doctors, and research into new forms of treatment. They are not, therefore, independent of collective welfare in practice. These private services give their rich users a false picture of this underlying interdependency, however, and, more importantly perhaps, give them a reduced incentive to support investment in wider public provision.

• At the bottom end, those experiencing poverty and social exclusion may be unable to benefit most effectively from the public services on which they do rely, especially where these are being run down by lack of investment. Many of the worst performing schools, with fewer pupils achieving good GCSE grades for instance, are in the most deprived areas. And in places like these local people (without private transport) will also be dependent on public transport to access anything but very local services. As O'Hara (2015) graphically revealed, those struggling on low wages and inadequate benefits at the bottom of our unequal social order are generally those most dependent upon public services, but least able to benefit fully from them.

Collective investment in public goods and services thus needs to be accompanied by strategic intervention to reduce extreme inequalities, if our creation of the common good is to be owned and enjoyed equally by all.

Rethinking public services

The provision of public services is often associated with the twentieth-century development of state welfare and the creation of the welfare state. In this, services are provided for all by public agencies whose job it is to deliver them to all who need them. The assumption was that comprehensive provision and protection meant monopoly control by public agencies dedicated to providing services. As argued in Chapter 4, however, this led, to some extent at least, to a 'provider culture' in public services, in which producer interests could become dominant over user interests, with queues, forms, regulations and bureaucracy all creating an impression that these were not our services, but something that we had to apply for, and which would be provided to us in a prescribed form, if at all.

This is perhaps a rather harsh characterisation of state services, not least as many public service workers are dedicated 'knights' rather than self-serving 'knaves' – to use Le Grand's (2003) terminology.

But the problem of producer control is a real one, especially where it leads to a lack of engagement and ownership of public services by those who need them, and pay for them.

The criticisms of the provider culture have already resulted in a series of reforms to public services designed, in theory at least, to make these more accessible and accountable. These include the new public management (NPM) introduction of targets and inspections, the moves towards personalisation and co-production, and the encouragement of alternative providers, as discussed in Chapter 4. These changes have moved welfare provision from the monopoly and bureaucratic services of the twentieth century towards the 'third way', mixed economy of the early twenty-first.

There has been much discussion, especially in public management, about the need to rethink the provision of public services to respond to the problems of the provider culture (see Griffiths et al, 2013; and more generally Flynn, 2012). Often this has focused on a shift from inputs (who provides what services?) to outcomes (how do users benefit from the services they receive?). This focus on outcomes has accompanied the target setting of NPM and the opening up of public services to alternative private and third sector providers. If what matters is how people benefit, then this can be specified in the design of services and built into the criteria for establishing or commissioning them. Then any provider who can guarantee to meet these outcomes could be commissioned to deliver the service.

There are potential advantages in this outcome focus for the users of public services. What matters is what they get, not who provides it. However, there are potential problems too with a focus only on user benefits, especially only on the benefits to individuals. How services are delivered also matters, and can in practice determine who benefits from them. One of the criticisms of the provider culture has been its (relative) lack of concern with the accessibility of services (the nine to five opening hours of local offices), as discussed in Chapter 4. Alternative providers can deliver accessible services, of course, but a focus only on outcomes does not guarantee this. In particular, this is likely to be the case where payment for the service provided is based only on outcome measures, as the Coalition government's Work Programme revealed – see Box 8.1.

Box 8.1 The Work Programme

In 2011 the UK government decided to transfer the employment support for long-term unemployed people to alternative providers, who would be commissioned to deliver this to clients referred to them by the state agencies, Jobcentre Plus. Payment for these contracts was based on the results achieved by the contractors in placing clients in employment. This meant that only large private sector companies were able to take on these contracts, as significant capital was needed to underwrite the services until the outcome-based payments were received. Smaller third sector providers were therefore largely excluded. It also meant that many of the providers concentrated their efforts mainly on support for those most likely to get jobs, as here the outcomes were easier to achieve, leaving some of the most excluded people with the most limited job prospects receiving only minimal support – what some critics called 'creaming and parking' (Rees at al, 2013).

Accessibility of services could be included in commissioning, but it is more difficult to specify this than more measurable outcomes. What is more, the guarantee that alternative providers will ultimately deliver on all the specified elements of service contracts is problematic where these are private companies or third sector organisations, whose long-term future may be uncertain and whose only formal commitment to public services is the (temporary) contract specification to which they are working. As mentioned in Chapter 4, it is only state agencies that have a mandate, and a responsibility, to provide for all citizens, and it is state agencies who in practice will provide the back-up to alternative providers, should these fail to survive or deliver. There is a place for alternative providers for some services, in some circumstances, at some times, but these can never be a replacement for state responsibility for ensuring that services are available and accessible to all, and for stepping in to alter or revoke contracts where these fail – see Box 8.2.

Box 8.2 Kids Company

Kids Company was a charity founded in 1996 to provide support for deprived and vulnerable inner-city children. From a small drop-in centre in South London it expanded to include a range of centres in London and Bristol, and by 2011 claimed that it was supporting around 36,000 children a year. It was popular with both the Labour and Coalition governments as a leading example of innovative alternative service provision. It received significant support from government amounting to over £42 million, as well as support from a range of prominent donors. Shortly after receiving a further £3 million from the Cabinet Office in 2015, however, the charity got into serious financial difficulties and went into almost immediate liquidation. The centres were all closed and the young people who had been receiving support had to turn to hard-pressed local state services as the only provider of last resort, although in practice the numbers involved were far less than the Kids Company publicity had suggested.

Finally, and most importantly, public services require public investment, whoever designs or delivers them. For the reasons explored above, we cannot rely on private markets to supply public goods. This is also the case for third sector organisations, like Kids Company, whose mission is inevitably limited and who do not have a mandate to represent or invest in all citizens. Only the state can act collectively on behalf of all citizens to make the financial investments that underpin the provision of public goods and services. Taxation and public spending may appear unpopular, and they may in neoliberal discourse run counter to individual choice and market competition. But for public services to provide the public goods that will meet the needs of all citizens, collective investment must be undertaken by the state. As argued at the beginning of this chapter, a welfare society needs a welfare state.

The common good

Taxation and public spending are a collective investment in public goods and services. Taken together they constitute the common good that we share as members of our society. This common good is much more than the private goods that we could acquire through our own resources. When you get the train to your nearby hospital, just think what it would have cost to buy this infrastructure and expertise as an individual each time you might need it. There is also more to the common good than the individual benefits derived by individual service users. For instance, public health and education benefits us all: if I am immunised against an infectious disease, it helps to prevent this spreading to others too; if I can read and write and use communication technology, I can communicate with others and they can communicate with me. These public benefits extend to social security protection too, which means that older workers can retire and open up jobs to younger people, and that unemployed workers can be supported and retrained so that they are able to occupy new roles in our changing economy.

Our collective investment in the common good is also cumulative. It is previous generations of taxpayers who have invested in the roads, schools and hospitals that we now rely on. We enjoy the legacy left to us by our forebears, as most of us brought up following the creation of the welfare state in the mid twentieth century are acutely aware. We must also therefore leave a legacy of common good to our descendants with continuing investment in infrastructure and human capital – the schools and teachers that our children's children will need. However, there has also been much public debate in recent years about the more problematic longer-term legacies that we might be leaving too – the accumulated deficits in our public expenditure, and the impact of our continued reliance on fossil fuels on our climate and the global environment.

At the end of 2014 public sector net debt in the UK was £1,483 billion (or £1.4 trillion, 80.9 per cent of GDP), and the government was paying £46 billion a year in interest payments on this outstanding debt (ONS, 2015). This is higher than in the previous three decades, but not by longer-term comparison. At the end of the Second World War public debt was over 220 per cent of GDP, and it was over 150 per cent for most of the first half of the last century, only dropping below 100 per cent in the early 1960s – see Figure 8.1. Our ability to pay down our public debts, as is the case with our private ones, depends on our future economic circumstances, as the rapid decline in debt after the 1960s revealed. Yet the Conservative government of 2015 committed itself to removing public sector debt as the overriding priority for political and economic planning, and the justification for draconian cuts in public services.

Our environmental legacy is much less under the control of the UK (or any) national government, for it is global omissions of carbons and other pollutants which determine climate change.

Figure 8.1 UK national debt as a percentage of GDP

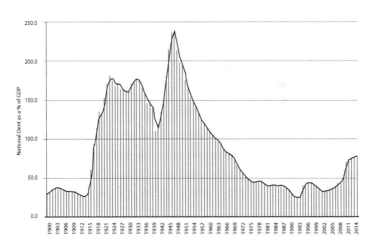

Source: www.economicshelp.org/blog/11697/debt/post-war-boom

As discussed in Chapter 7, these do provide a changing, and challenging, context for future economic planning. In response to this UK governments have set targets for reductions in omissions here, and the country has also been party to international agreements on global environmental change including the major international conference in Paris in December 2015 – although whether these will be sufficient to halt or reverse damaging climate change remains contested.

It is the positive legacy of investment in our common good, rather than the negative legacies of public debt and climate change, that should be the focus for the planning of welfare provision, however. This does mean that debt reduction and environmental improvement do not matter – of course they do. But these are part of the broader context in which we must plan a positive legacy for the common good, not an excuse for not doing so.

Writing about the common good in the US, Sievers (2010) argued that it should be understood as the consequence of the balance that must be struck between our individual and our social needs. He also linked it to the operation of civil society. In this sense, it is the common good that binds us all in society and is at the core of our social relations, indeed, of our collective humanity. Through acting collectively as social beings we can create much more than we ever could as individuals.

At key moments in history we can see this collective commitment to the common good revealed in political discourse and social change. This was most obviously the case in the UK in the post-war period of the Labour government of 1945–51 and the creation of the welfare state. The country had just come through six years of total war, the most devastating and costly war in British (indeed world) history. The war had affected rich and poor alike – German bombing was not very discriminating. Citizens had had to work together to meet the war effort, stepping outside of traditional roles, with women drafted into manufacturing and working class children from the East End of London evacuated to rural villages. The government had had to intervene to organise and promote production of armaments and to guarantee the distribution of food and other household goods. Many of these items were rationed with the same entitlement for all, no matter what social status. In the Second World War, perhaps more so than ever before (or since) in UK history, people really were 'all in it together'. As Figure 8.1 reveals, this collective effort also led to a massive increase in public borrowing and the national debt, which peaked at the end of the war – far greater than the deficit we are now struggling with in the 2010s.

This collective effort provided a social and economic context for the collective welfare reforms introduced by the Labour government under Clement Attlee after the war. The welfare state was in a sense the 'reward' for Britain's collective commitment to fighting, and winning, the war. It was popular, and it was sustained by subsequent Conservative governments over the following two decades. The post-war welfare state was not without its faults, as I have discussed in this book, but it was evidence of popular support for public welfare, with Labour sweeping into victory in the 1945 election, despite the fact that the Conservatives were still led by Winston Churchill, who had just led the country to victory in the war. It was evidence too of political consensus on the need for public welfare, which even acquired its own shorthand, *Butskellism* – an amalgamation of the names of the Labour Chancellor of the Exchequer, Gaitskell, and his Conservative successor, Butler, which was coined by *The Economist* magazine to refer to the parties' shared commitments to the welfare state.

Popular support for collective welfare in the UK has certainly declined since those post-war years, with the survey evidence discussed in Chapter 7 suggesting that only around a third of people now express support for increases in taxation to fund additional spending on welfare. In 2015 the Conservative government that was elected has committed to cutting expenditure to reduce the public sector debt, in particular, through further cuts in social security benefits. This is underpinned by a neoliberal discourse which emphasises the freedom and responsibility of individuals, and demonises high taxation and government interference. What is more, it is accompanied by growing inequality, which has created an ever greater gap between the circumstances and experiences of those at opposite ends of the economic hierarchy.

A return to the collective spirit of 1945 does not seem likely 70 years on – though certainly no one is suggesting that we might need another war to bring us all together. However, there are some now arguing, and organising, to promote a reaffirmation of a collective commitment to the common good in twenty-first-century UK society. A group of third sector organisations, supported by the Carnegie Trust, have come together to promote 'a call to action for the common good' (Crowther, 2014). The New Economics Foundation (NEF) has published a pamphlet calling for moves 'towards a new social settlement' (Coote, 2015). And a collection of faith-based writers have produced a collection of papers containing a plea to work 'together for the common good' (Sagovsky and McGrail, 2015).

This is recognised by academic commentators too. Atkinson (2015) and Piketty (2014) have argued for the need for greater equality, Hills (2015) for the need for the redistribution of resources, and Taylor-Gooby (2013) for the need for a new political economy of the welfare state. Behind all of these is a belief that to challenge the individualism of neoliberalism, we need to recognise again the benefits that we all receive from collective investment in the common good, and the continued importance of individual interests being bound into the production and use of public goods and services. The arguments are there; how can they be translated into political action and policy change?

Civil society and collective action

The UK welfare state was based on the commitment to the provision of public services through the actions of state agencies. As I have argued, however, it has always been accompanied by a mixed economy of welfare, with a range of different providers delivering different aspects of welfare support. This is true of the welfare states in continental Europe too, and of welfare provision across the developed world in the Americas and Asia. What these other regimes reveal is that the balance between different providers is different in different national settings, with informal and family welfare playing a greater part in many Asian welfare regimes and private market providers occupying a more central role in the US.

In all welfare regimes there is a balance between these different fields of provision. Even when we talk about welfare states, we are usually referring to a wider public sphere of welfare provision, of which formal delivery by the state is only one part. This wider sphere of public action has sometimes been referred to as *civil society*. Sievers (2010) has discussed the history of the use of the concept, linking it to collective activity to promote the common good, particularly in the US, and Powell (2007) has explored the wider political and conceptual debates about civil society and its relationship with the development of democracy and the welfare state.

In Europe the term has sometimes been used to refer to the third sector, and the UK government has recently established an Office for Civil Society to coordinate policy for what they call 'civil society organisations'. However, this narrower focus is challenged by some European commentators, such as Evers (2013), who has argued that the use of civil society as a synonym for third sector organisations is only one dimension of the use of the term, and a rather narrow one at that.

A wider discourse on civil society and its relationship to collective action, both nationally and internationally, and to democratic government and civic participation can be found in the articles in an international journal on the topic, the *Journal of Civil Society*. However, perhaps the leading commentator on and proponent for civil society is Michael Edwards, a UK academic and activist based in the US who has previously worked for the World Bank and the Ford Foundation, and who has written an influential book on the subject, now in its third edition (Edwards, 2014).

Edwards argues that there are the distinctive, though overlapping discourses on civil society:

- civil society as associational life – where we participate in formal and informal organisations;
- civil society as the good society – where we debate what values should inform social relations;
- civil society as the public sphere – where all public action and debate takes place.

These are different because, as Edwards explains, civil society is a contested concept, with different proponents employing different definitions, and invoking it to support or promote different social and political objectives, as Powell (2007) also explores. Edwards does not promote any one of these discourses in particular; indeed, his broader point is that we should be alert to the strengths and weaknesses of each, while also recognising the importance of the concept in informed debate and practice within each. Taken together, however, they embrace an approach to civil society that includes the interaction of the state, the market and the third sector in promoting associational activity, progressive social relations and a vibrant public sphere.

The importance of civil society for Edwards is that it can, and should, inform policy and practice across these spheres; here his account of civil society is at its heart a normative one. Civil society discourse should focus on how we can act together to make our world a better place. In the final chapter on 'What is to be done' he argues that civil society is the critical focus for collective action in society, providing a vehicle for associational activity, promoting participation of citizens in public life and underpinning the successful operation of democratic government. He argues that, 'Civil society is simultaneously a goal to aim for, a means to achieve it, and a framework for engaging with each other about ends and means' (Edwards, 2014, pp 129–30).

What is clear is that Edwards sees civil society as more than just third sector organisations, or associational life, as his first discourse has it, and this has been taken up by others such as Evers (2013). Civil society also includes the state, and in particular it encompasses the *interdependence* of the state and other sectors of social and economic activity. This includes the market too, and some have argued that we should recognise here the potential for the creation of a *civil economy* alongside civil society. Commercial companies rely directly and indirectly on the state, for regulation, for public contracts and subsidies, for infrastructure like roads and railways, and for the general welfare of their workers. They can also make significant contributions to the wider common good, indirectly by encouraging their employees to engage in voluntary activity in the UK through vehicles like Business in the Community, and directly, as the Cadbury and Rowntree chocolate makers did in the twentieth century, by providing supportive social and cultural environments for their workers and their local communities (see Cadbury, 2010). Such civil economy commitments can be part of a broader conception of civil society as the site for all action which promotes public, or collective, goods.

For Edwards, and for other proponents of civil society, therefore, it is a 'good' – indeed, it is a public good. It provides the scope for the positive experience of collective action – we want to work together with others. It provides a variety of organisational forms to deliver this – we can work together in voluntary organisations, in campaigning groups, in commercial companies and in state agencies. It provides a public space for debate and deliberation over the ends and means of collective investment – we can challenge or petition our politicians and policy makers, or even become policy makers or politicians ourselves. It is for these reasons that proponents like the Carnegie Trust group (Crowther, 2014) link participation in civil society with the promotion of the common good.

Civil society is also a normative concept. What we mean by civil society and how to achieve this are part of our understanding of what it is. In this sense, promoting civil society is making the case for the 'good society', and this is where it can become an essential element of a renewed discourse on the case for collective investment in welfare and the promotion of the common good. Civil society is the *means* for achieving collective action and promoting the importance of associational activity; but is also the *ends* to which we aspire through this collective activity. We all want, or we should want, to be members of a civil society – a civil society in which all have the capability to participate and to flourish, a civil society in which we invest collectively in our welfare and our future welfare, and a civil society in which our common good is greater than our individual interests.

The desire to live in a civil society thus provides us with a goal to challenge the neoliberal discourse of individual freedom and market competition. It provides the means to achieve this through associational activity and participation in the public sphere. It provides the ideological framework though which we can articulate the need for investment in the common good. It provides the answer to the question of why we need welfare: we need it because it is what makes our society civil.

Summary

The creation of the welfare state in the mid twentieth century was the product of popular support for and belief in collective investment in public services provided through the state to promote the common good. The welfare state was never the monopoly provider culture that some critics accused it of being, however. We have always had something of a mixed economy of welfare – what some have called a welfare society. But what the analysis developed in this book reveals, is that the welfare state and the welfare society are interdependent, not mutually exclusive. This is because private markets and voluntary action could never meet our needs for public goods without public investment and state action. This interdependence can be captured, and promoted, by an understanding of and commitment to *civil society* as the place where individual actors meet collective organisation – or, to use the sociological categories that

I introduced in Chapter 1, where agents meet structures. Civil society also provides a normative base for collective action – we act together to make our society a better place where all can flourish.

Key texts

Taylor-Gooby (2013), as mentioned before, is a good guide to the political and economic challenges facing the welfare state in the early twenty-first century, and what we will need to do to meet these. Glennerster (2003) explains the economic case for the provision of public welfare and how this is paid for, and Sandel (2012) provides a wide-ranging and accessible discussion of the limits of markets. Sievers (2010) summarises the history of the development of debates about civil society over several centuries, and Powell (2007) provides a useful guide to conceptual debates on this. Edwards (2014) is an accessible and engaging review of its enduring importance.

References

Alcock, P. (2006) *Understanding poverty* (3rd edn), Basingstoke: Palgrave.

Alcock, P. with May, M. (2014) *Social policy in Britain* (4th edn), Basingstoke: Palgrave.

Alcock, P., Glennerster, H., Oakley, A. and Sinfield, A. (eds) (2001) *Welfare and wellbeing: Richard Titmuss's contribution to social policy*, Bristol: Policy Press.

Alcock, P., Haux, T., May, M. and Wright, S. (eds) (2016) *The student's companion to social policy* (5th edn), Chichester: Wiley-Blackwell.

Atkinson, A.B. (2015) *Inequality: What can be done?*, Cambridge, MA: Harvard University Press.

Audit Commission (2013) *Income from charging: Using data from Value for Money Profiles, September 2013*, London: Audit Commission.

Bacon, R. and Eltis, W. (1976) *Britain's economic problem: Too few producers*, London: Macmillan.

Baldock, J., Mitton, L., Manning, N. and Vickerstaff, S. (eds) (2011) *Social policy* (4th edn), Oxford: Oxford University Press.

Ball, S. (2008) *The education debate* (2nd edn), Bristol: Policy Press.

Beck, U. (1992) *Risk society: Towards a new modernity*, London: Sage.

Beresford, P., Fleming, J., Glynn, M., Bewley, C., Croft, S., Branfield, F. and Postle, K. (2011) *Supporting people: Towards a person-centred approach*, Bristol: Policy Press.

Beveridge, Sir W. (1942) *Report on social insurance and allied services*, Cmd 6404, London: HMSO.

Brighouse, H. (2004) *Justice*, Cambridge: Polity Press.

Booth, C. (1889) *The life and labour of the people*, London: Williams and Northgate.

Borrie, G. (1994), *Social justice: Strategies for national renewal: The report of the Commission on Social Justice*, London: Vintage.

Boyle, D. (2001) *The tyranny of numbers: Why counting cannot make us happy*, New York: Falmingo/Harper Collins.

Bradshaw, J. (1972) 'The taxonomy of social need', in G. McLachlan (ed) *Problems and progress in medical care*, Oxford: Oxford University Press.

Butcher, T. (2002) *Delivering welfare* (2nd edn), Milton Keynes: Open University Press.

Cadbury, D. (2010) *Chocolate wars: From Cadbury to Kraft, 200 years of sweet success and bitter rivalry*, London: Harper Press.

Campbell, J. and Oliver, M. (1996) *Disability politics: Understanding our past, changing our future*, London: Routledge.

Cameron, D. (2009) *'The Big Society'*, Hugo Young Memorial Lecture, 10 November 2009, Guardian Offices, London.

Castles, F. (1999) *Comparative public policy: Patterns of post war transformation*, Cheltenham: Edward Elgar.

Castles, F. (2004) *The future of the welfare state*, Oxford: Oxford University Press.

Clarke, J., Newman, J., Smith, N., Vidler, E. and Westmarland, L. (2007) *Creating citizen-consumers: Changing publics and changing public services*, London: Sage.

Clarke, M. and Stewart, J. (1988) *The enabling council*, London: Local Government Management Board.

Coote, A. (2015) *People, planet, power: Towards a new social settlement*, London: New Economics Foundation (NEF).

Craig, G., Atkin, K., Chattoo, S. and Flynn, R. (2012) *Understanding race and ethnicity: Theory, history, policy, practice*, Bristol: Policy Press.

Crompton, R. (2008) *Class and stratification: An introduction to current debates* (3rd edn), Cambridge: Polity Press.

Crowther, N. (2014) *A call to action for the common good*, London: Carnegie UK Trust.

Daly, M. (2011) *Welfare*, Cambridge: Polity Press.

Deacon, A. and Bradshaw, J. (1983) *Reserved for the poor: The means-test in British social policy*, Oxford: Basil Blackwell and Martin Robertson.

Deacon, B. (2007) *Global social policy and governance*, London: Sage.

Deakin, N. and Wright, A. (eds) (1990) *Consuming public services*, London: Routledge.

Dean, H. (2012) *Social Policy* (2nd edn), Cambridge: Polity Press.

Department for Work and Pensions (DWP) and Office for Disability Issues (2012) *Disability facts and figures*, London: DWP.

Dolowitz, D. (1998) *Learning from America: Policy transfer and the development of the British workfare state*, Brighton: Sussex Academic Press.

Doyal, L and Gough, I. (1991) *A theory of human need*, Basingstoke: Palgrave Macmillan.

Edwards, M. (2014) *Civil society* (3rd edn), Cambridge: Polity Press.

Ellison, N. (2006) *The transformation of welfare states?*, London: Routledge.

Esping-Andersen, G. (1990) *The three worlds of welfare capitalism*, Cambridge: Polity Press.

Finch, J. and Groves, D. (eds) (1983) *A labour of love: Women, work and caring*, London: Routledge and Kegan Paul.

Evers, A. (2013) 'The concept of "civil society": different understandings and their implications for third sector policies', *Voluntary Sector Review*, 4(2): 49–64.

Fitzpatrick, T. (2001) *Welfare theory: An introduction*, Basingstoke: Palgrave.

Ftizpatrick, T. (2005) *New theories of welfare*, Basingstoke: Palgrave.

Fitzpatrick, T. (ed) (2011) *Understanding the environment and social policy*, Bristol: Policy Press.

Flaherty, D. (2011) 'The vaccine-autism connection: a public health crisis caused by unethical medical practices and fraudulent science', *The Annals of Pharmacotherapy*, 45: 1302–4.

Flynn, N. (2012) *Public sector management* (6th edn), London: Sage.

Giddens, A. (1990) *The consequences of modernity*, Cambridge: Polity Press.

Giddens, A. and Pierson, C. (1998) *Conversations with Anthony Giddens: Making sense of modernity*, Stanford, CA: Stanford University Press.

Glennerster, H. (1997) *Paying for welfare: Towards 2000* (3rd edn), Harlow: Prentice Hall.

Glennerster, H. (2007) *British social policy: 1945 to the present* (3rd edn), Oxford: Basil Blackwell.

Glennerster, H. (2009) *Understanding the finance of social policy: What welfare costs and how to pay for it* (2nd edn), Bristol: Policy Press.

Golding, P. and Middleton, S. (1982) *Images of welfare: Press and public attitudes to welfare*, Oxford: Basil Blackwell and Martin Robertson.

Griffiths, S., Kippin, H. and Stoker, G. (eds) (2013) *Public services: A new reform agenda*, London: Bloomsbury Press.

Hantrais, L. (2007) *Social policy in the European Community* (3rd edn), Basingstoke: Palgrave.

Hay, C. and Wincott, D. (2012) *The political economy of European welfare capitalism*, Basingstoke: Palgrave.

Hills, J. (2015) *Good times, bad times: The welfare myth of them and us*, Bristol: Policy Press.

Hirschman, A. (1970) *Exit, voice and loyalty: Responses to decline in firms, organisations and states*, Cambridge, MA: Harvard University Press.

Hirst, P. (1994) *Associative democracy*, Cambridge: Polity Press.

HM Treasury (2015) *Budget 2015*, HC1093, London: HM Treasury.

Hunter, D. (2008) *The health debate*, Bristol: Policy Press.

Hutton, W. (1995) *The state we're in*, London: Jonathan Cape.

Hutton, W. (2002) *The world we're in*, London: Little Brown.

Hutton, W. (2013) *The state to come*, London: Vintage Books.

Kane, D. et al (2015) *UK civil society almanac 2015*, London: National Council for Voluntary Organisations.

Keynes, J. M. (1936) *The general theory of employment, interest and money*, London: Macmillan.

Le Grand, J. (1982) *The strategy of equality: Redistribution and the social services*, London: Allen & Unwin.

Le Grand, J. (2003) *Motivation, agency and public policy: Of knights and knaves, pawns and queens*, Oxford: Oxford University Press.

Le Grand, J. and Bartlett, W. (eds) (1993) *Quasi-markets and social policy*, Basingstoke: Macmillan.

Lewis, O. (1965) *The children of Sanchez*, Harmondsworth: Penguin.

Lewis, O. (1968) *La vida*, London: Panther.

Lodge, G. and Schmuecker, K. (eds) (2010) *Devolution in practice 2010*, London: Institute for Public Policy Research.

Mack, J. and Lansley, S. (1985) *Poor Britain*, London: George Allen and Unwin.

Mack, J. and Lansley, S. (2015) *Breadline Britain: The rise of mass poverty*, London: Oneworld Publications.

Marshall, T.H. (1950) *Citizenship and social class*, Cambridge: Cambridge University Press.

Marx, K. (1869) *The eighteenth brumaire of Louis Bonaparte*, Moscow: Progress Publishers.

McKenzie, L. (2015) *Getting by: Estates, class and culture in austerity Britain*, Bristol: Policy Press.

Miller, C. (2004), *Producing welfare: A modern agenda*, Basingstoke: Palgrave.

Mishra, R. (1999) *Globalisation and the Welfare State*, Aldershot: Edward Elgar.

Morel, N., Palier, B. and Palme, J. (eds) (2011) *Towards a social investment welfare state? Ideas, policies and challenges*, Bristol: Policy Press.

Mulgan, G. and Bury, F. (eds) (2006) *Double devolution: The renewal of local government*, London: The Smith Institute.

Needham, C. (ed) (2011) *Personalising public services: Understanding the personalisation narrative*, Bristol: Policy Press.

Needham, C. and Glasby, J. (2014) *Debates in personalisation*, Bristol: Policy Press.

Newman, J. (2001) *Modernising governance: New Labour, policy and society*, London: Sage.

Nussbaum, M. (2011) *Creating capabilities: The human development approach*, Cambridge, MA: Belknap/Harvard University Press.

Office for Budget Responsibility (2015) *Economic and fiscal outlook: March 2105*, Cm 9024, London: HM Stationery Office.

Office for National Statistics (ONS) (2010) *National population projections, 2010-based projections*, London: ONS.

ONS (2012) *Statistical bulletin: 2011 census: Key statistics for England and Wales, March 2011*, London: ONS.

ONS (2013) *Summary results, 2012-based national population projections*, London: ONS.

ONS (2014) *The effects of taxes and benefits on household income, 2012/13*, London: ONS.

ONS (2015) *Summary: Public finance figures, April 2015*, London: ONS.

O'Hara, M. (2015) *Austerity bites: A journey to the sharp end of cuts in the UK*, Bristol: Policy Press.

Oliver, M. (2009) *Understanding disability: From theory to practice* (2nd edn), Basingstoke: Palgrave.

Osborne, S., Radnor, Z. and Nasi, G. (2013) 'A new theory for public service management: towards a (public) service-dominant approach', *American Review of Public Administration*, 43(2): 135–58.

Pascall, G. (2012) *Gender equality in the welfare state*, Bristol: Policy Press.

Payne, G. (ed) (2013) *Social divisions* (3rd edn), Basingstoke: Palgrave.

Pierson, C. (1998) *Beyond the welfare state: The new political economy of welfare* (2nd edn), Cambridge: Polity Press.

Piketty, T. (2014) *Capital in the twenty-first century*, Cambridge, MA: Harvard University Press.

Platt, L. (2011) *Understanding inequalities: Stratification and difference*, Cambridge: Polity Press.

Pollitt, C. (1990) *Managerialism and the public services*, Oxford: Basil Blackwell.

Powell, F. (2007) *The politics of civil society: Big Society and small government* (2nd edn), Bristol: Policy Press.

Rawls, J. (1999) *A theory of justice* (revised edn), Oxford: Oxford University Press.

Rees, J., Whitworth, A. and Carter, E. (2013) *Support for all in the work programme? Different payments, same old problem*, TSRC Working Paper 115, Birmingham: Third Sector Research Centre (TSRC).

Roberts, K. (2011) *Class in modern Britain* (2nd edn), Basingstoke: Palgrave.

Room, G. (ed) (1995) *Beyond the threshold: The measurement and analysis of social exclusion*, Bristol: Policy Press.

Room, G. et al (1993) *Anti-poverty action research in Europe*, Bristol: School of Advanced Urban Studies, University of Bristol.

Rowntree, B.S. (1901) *Poverty: A study of town life*, London: Macmillan.

Runciman, W.G. (1966) *Relative deprivation and social justice: A study of attitudes to social inequality in twentieth-century England*, Harmondsworth: Penguin.

Sagovsky, N. and McGrail, P. (eds) (2015) *Together for the common good: Towards a national conversation*, London: SCM Press.

Sandel, M. (2012) *What money can't buy: The moral limits of markets*, London: Allen Lane.

Sayer, A. (2014) *Why we can't afford the rich*, Bristol: Policy Press.

Seligman, M. (2011) *Flourish: A visionary new understanding of happiness and wellbeing*, New York: Free Press.

Sen, A. (2009) *The idea of justice*, Cambridge, MA: Harvard University Press.

Shah, S. and Priestley, M. (2011) *Disability and social change: Private lives and public places*, Bristol: Policy Press.

Sievers, B. (2010) *Civil society, philanthropy and the fate of the commons*, Hanover, NH: Tufts University Press.

Spicker, P. (2007) *The idea of poverty*, Bristol: Policy Press.

Stoker, G. (1991) *The politics of local government* (2nd edn), Basingstoke: Macmillan.

Stoker, G. (2006) *Why politics matters: Making democracy work*, Basingstoke: Palgrave.

Tawney, R.H. (1913) 'Inaugural Lecture: "Poverty as an Industrial Problem"', reproduced in *Memoranda on the problems of poverty, Vol. 2*, London: William Morris Press.

Taylor, M. (2011) *Public policy in the community* (2nd edn), Basingstoke: Palgrave.

Taylor-Gooby, P. (2013) *The double crisis of the welfare state and what we can do about it*, Basingstoke: Palgrave Pivot.

Taylor-Gooby, P. and Taylor, E. (2015) *British social attitudes 32: Benefits and welfare*, London: NatCen Social Research.

Thaler, R. and Sunstein, C. (2008) *Nudge: Improving decisions about health, wealth and happiness*, New Haven, CT: Yale University Press.

Therborn, G. and Roebroek, J. (1986). 'The irreversible welfare state: its recent maturation, its encounter with the economic crisis, and its future prospects', *International Journal of Health Services*, *16*(3): 319–38.

Timmins, N. (2001) *The five giants: A biography of the welfare state* (rev. edn), London: HarperCollins.

Townsend, P. (1979) *Poverty in the United Kingdom: A survey of household resources and standards of living*, Harmondsworth: Penguin.

Toynbee, P. and Walker, D. (2015) *Cameron's coup: How the Tories took Britain to the brink*, London: Guardian Books.

Unwin, J. (2013) *Why fight poverty?*, London Publishing Partnership.

Webb, S. (1911) *The necessary basis of society*, Fabian Tract 159, London: Fabian Society.

White Paper (2011) *Open public services*, Cm 845, London: HM Stationery Office.

White, S. (2007) *Equality*, Cambridge: Polity Press.

Wilkinson, R. and Pickett, K. (2009) *The spirit level: Why more equal societies almost always do better*, London: Allen Lane.

Williams, F. (1989) *Social policy: A critical introduction*, Cambridge: Polity Press.

Wilson, E. (1977) *Women and the welfare state*, London: Tavistock.

Wright Mills, C. (2000) *The sociological imagination* (40th anniversary edn), Oxford: Oxford University Press.

Yeates, N. (ed) (2008) *Understanding global social policy*, Bristol: Policy Press.

Index

References to boxes and figures are in *italics*